WHAT IS 1

WHAT IS

PRAYER?

Dunstan Adams OSB
Monk of Ampleforth

Ampleforth Abbey
(Distributed by Gracewing)

AMPLEFORTH ABBEY
YORK YO62 4EN
from
Gracewing
Southern Avenue, Leominster
Herefordshire HR6 0QF

ISBN 0 85244 502 4

*Typeset at Ampleforth Abbey in 12pt/14.5pt
Monotype Bembo with 15pt Perpetua capitals*

Printed by Redwood Books
Trowbridge, Wiltshire BA14 8RN

CONTENTS

PART ONE

Preface   *i*

Introduction
   Origen's Preface to his treatise 'On Prayer'   *1*

Section One
   Our Lord, Man of Prayer   *3*

Section Two
   We attempt to pray   *19*

Section Three
   Some examples from others:

   1) *The 'Theology' of Prayer from Revelations
      of Divine Love by Julian of Norwich*   *54*

   2) *Some examples from 1st to 20th centuries. It
      should be recognisable that it is the Pray-er
      rather than the prayers. So all the examples share:*

      i) *a personal one-to-One relationship,*

      ii) *based on the Incarnation, therefore always
          individual and constantly communal because,*

      iii) *Trinitarian.*   *59*

PART TWO

Section Four
   What Next?   82

Conclusion
   His atonement is for our at-One-ment even now.
   Do I believe this? Help my unbelief.   112

ACKNOWLEDGEMENTS

Gospel refs taken from either *JB 1967 edition*, or *Catholic RSV*, or *Revised English Bible 1989 edition*, or *Knox*, or *own free adaptations.*

St John of the Cross, *Poems*. Translation from Penguin Books 1968

Julian of Norwich, *Revelations of Divine Love*, Penguin Books 1966.

TS Eliot, Faber & Faber 1970.

I am deeply indebted to the Carmelites of Wood Hall for their generous support of prayers; and for reading the draft of this book and for making helpful comments. However the interpretation remains the sole responsibility of the author.

PREFACE

Whenever we recognise the Word incarnate as primarily Man of Prayer we are drawn to experience, in Christ, union in prayer. We are no longer on our own. *What is Prayer?* offers not an analytical answer but an awareness of an ever present need:

> Father, as your Son would pray in me,
> so I would pray to you.

Such a need, intimately personal yet always communal, is expressed by the quotations and comments in the middle section of *What is Prayer?*

This exposition of the question follows a classical development. There is a recognisable beginning, middle and end. Each part is causally connected to the next. The 'end' can only reach full term in and with the ascended Man of Prayer at the end of time.

Meanwhile, the theme from beginning to end is simply let us pray. The great Doctor of Prayer, St Teresa of Avila writes in the *Book of her Life:*

> Prayer in my opinion, is nothing else than a close sharing between friends; it means taking time... to be with Him who we know loves us.

And in her *Way of Perfection* we read:

> I do not ask you to meditate on Him, nor to produce
> great thoughts, nor to feel deep devotion: I only ask
> you to look at Him. (*Way of Perfection 26.3*)

Let us now look at Him in prayer as Man of Prayer.

PART ONE

In second century Origen's Preface to *On Prayer* we read:

> The discussion of prayer is so great a task that it
> requires the Father to reveal it, his Firstborn Word to
> teach it, and the Spirit to enable us to think and speak
> rightly of so great a subject. That is why I, who am
> only a human being and in no way attribute an under-
> standing of prayer to myself, think it right to pray for
> the Spirit before beginning.

So, let us pray:

> Come, Holy Spirit, fill the hearts of Your faithful,
> and enkindle in them the fire of Your Love.
> Send forth Your Spirit and they shall be created.
> And You shall renew the face of the earth...

And again we pray:

> O God, who taught the hearts of the faithful
> by the Light of the Holy Spirit,
> grant that by the gift of the same Spirit

we may be always truly wise
and ever rejoice in His consolation.
We make our prayer through Christ our Lord.

Let us, now, look at our Lord as Man of Prayer, keeping
in mind His example and teaching.

Surely this is the very beginning of seeing how His
atonement for us gives us at-One-ment with His Father
and our Father in the Holy Spirit.

As we know, the Word incarnate came to dwell with
us because

God loved us first (*I Jn 4.10ff*)

and the nature of that Love is to communicate. That is
why He is called Emmanuel, God-with-us.

Our Lady's

> Be it done unto me according to your word (*Lk 1.26*)

means that the life of the Word in the flesh begins, in the spirit of prayer, as Redeemer in the womb. So, at His birth the heavenly host proclaims,

> Glory to God in the highest and to all of good-will, peace on earth! (*Lk 2.14*)

This embryonic prayer of mutual loving acceptance translates Mother and Child, and consequently us, if we will, into the ever-present *now* of God's Love. Nature and grace, time and eternity become for ever one. This is the wonderful ever-renewing Union brought about by the Incarnation of the Word. It cannot be undone. It is *now* and this *now* is for ever. The embryonic nature of this form of prayer is affirmed by God the Father at the baptism of His Son:

> Now when all the people were baptized, and when Jesus also had been baptized and was praying, the heavens opened, and the Holy Spirit descended upon Him

3

in bodily form, as a dove, and a voice came from heaven 'You are my beloved Son, in You I delight. (*Lk 3.21*)

God delights in the prayerful action of His Son as Man of prayer making atonement for us into at-One-ment. Only within such an Union can we be 'at home' with God.

The four evangelists often note that Jesus prays. Wherever He goes, whatever He does, He is in communication with God by prayer.

In St Luke's Gospel, the 'Gospel of Prayer', three references, as given above, namely to the Annunciation, the Nativity, and the Baptism, lead us to recognise that our Lord is first and foremost a Man of Prayer.

It is this personal communing with God rather than any miracles which follow from His prayer that makes him our Saviour from the consequences of sin and death.

It was this freely chosen priority for prayer which enabled Him to seek the will of the Father, and then to act in loving obedience, that reconciles us to Him and our Father.

It is His living in the Spirit of prayer that causes evil spirits and dis-eased consciences, instinctively, to cry out against Him so that even the forces of darkness witness to the power of His enlightening prayer.

4

Is this why He frequently requests those healed, by His prayer to the Father, to live in the Spirit of prayer rather than exult in their physical or psychological healing as such?

> As His reputation continued to grow, and large crowds would gather to hear Him and to have their sicknesses cured, He would always go off to some place where He could be alone and pray. (*Lk 5.15*)

Out on the hills,

> He spent the whole night in prayer to God before choosing the twelve apostles from among His disciples. (*Lk 6.12*)

And further on,

> Now one day when He was praying alone in the presence of His disciples, He put this question to them, 'Who do the crowds say I am?' (*Lk 9.18*)

Peter's declaration :

> You are the Christ

is confirmed by the subsequent Transfiguration –

> This is my Son, the Chosen One. Listen to Him.
> (*Lk 9.29*)

In the silence that followed, these words reverberate the Union manifest at His baptism. His priority for prayer grows upon those who watch Him at prayer. So, again,

> Once He was in a certain place praying and when He had finished one of His disciples, said, 'Lord, teach us to pray'…

and the 'Our Father' follows (*Lk 11.1ff*) with a full commentary on how prayer works, if we will share His example whether alone or in a congregation where everything, always, depends on being with Him in the Spirit of His prayer. It is this which alone saves our attempts at prayer from self-centred reverie.

> Simon, Simon! You must know Satan has got his wish to sift you all like wheat; but I have prayed for you, Simon, that your faith may not fail, and once you have recovered, you in your turn must strengthen your brothers…but I tell you Peter [*Cephas* rock]… you

will have denied three times that you know Me.
(*Lk 22.31*)

Without such an on-going, growing, awareness of the
infinite value of prayer there could have been no
Gethsemane prayer

— not my will but yours —

nor that last perfected prayer from the cross :

Father, forgive them… (*Lk 23.34*) *and*

Father, into your hands… (*Lk 23.46*)

That is the Spirit of the Man of Prayer — a Man of loving obedience, yet like us in all things but sin, especially
our sins of disobedience. Even so, He was tempted and
tried, like us, but He, even to fullest extremity of His perfect Humanity, even to death on the cross, so that with
Him we should recognise our hopeless weakness without Him. In this way, His Way, we recognise the Love of
God, manifest and at work in our midst simply because
he longs to share His Love with every receptive heart.
And this is the prayer of the Word made flesh in oneness-

with–us. In this we recognise that:

> All our hope lies in you alone. (*Ps 38*)

So we constantly pray:

> O God come to our aid,
> O Lord make haste to help us. (*Pss 39 & 69*)

Within this unique personal relationship we too are

> nearest to the Father's heart. (*Jn 1.18*)

Similar references to St Luke's account of our Lord as Man of Prayer may be found in St Matthew's and St Mark's gospels: reflectively, the accumulative affect is powerful. It is almost overwhelming in St John's account.

> In the Beginning was the Word… and the Word became flesh and dwelt amongst us… It is the only Son, Who is nearest to the Father's heart, Who has made Him known. (*Jn 1.1 ff*)

With St John's divine hindsight the synoptic 'Suffering Servant – the Man of Prayer' becomes '*Rex tremendæ majestatis*' (*Dies Iræ*) simply because He is the Truth of God.

> Yes, I am a king. I was born for this, I came into the world for this: to bear witness to the truth; and all who are on the side of truth listen to My voice. (*Jn 18.37*)

This is the voice of the Pray-er Who throughout the four gospels is first and foremost Man of Prayer. By His silent example and by His teaching, He constantly draws us to pray with Him for

> The truth will set you free. (*Jn 8.32*)

– free to see as He sees. Then in our weakness we can rejoice with Him, and all of good-will, in His saving Love…

> 'He Who sent Me… has not left Me to Myself' (*Jn 8.29*) … 'When you have lifted up the Son of Man, then you will know I am He'. (*Jn 8.28*)

Simultaneously, we can, like Martha and Mary feel despair *and* believe. At the same time as they weep for the death of their/our brother Lazarus, Martha says,

'Lord, *if only* you had been here, my brother would not have died'. (*Jn 11.21f*)

she also readily adds,

'Yes, I know but...' and, 'whatever You ask of God, He will grant You,'

And then Mary unwittingly echoes Martha's reproach,

'Lord, *if only* You had been here...'

Note, first, Christ prays :

'I thank You, Father, for hearing My prayer', *then*

'Lazarus, come out... unbind him, let him go free'. (*Jn 11.43*)

The Truth makes the way, His Way, clear, if we desire to follow. All that has been said or may ever be said about the primacy of His prayer is surely then made supremely manifest in His discourse at the Last Supper (*Jn 13-17*).

As Jesus approaches Jerusalem for the last time, with divine perception and perfect human intuition, He is fully aware of the rejoicing crowds and His heart responds but His soul is troubled (*Jn 12.27*). He can read the human heart better than we can. In Him there is no guile, no hidden double-think, no personal or political power struggle. The transparency of Light-in-darkness, must transcend the present historical moment of temptation.

A terrible trial of strength between the forces of good and evil faces Him with appalling clarity. In Himself, truly God and truly Man and therefore the only One Who can out-face the evil within the heart – core of our fallen, wounded, humanity, – He must freely and intimately identify Himself with our sinful state. The sinless One has to become sin (*II Cor 5.21*) to redeem us from the consequences of sin and death.

Only by dispossessing Himself of His awareness of His divinity (*Phil 2.5*) can the Immortal One of Infinite Love experience the full horror and fear of unredeemed death and demonstrate to us that by His resurrection from the dead we can recognise the fullness of the glory of His and our baptism for the remission of sins. Such is the stark fearful reality of the nature of His choice that He is tempted to pray,

'Father save Me from this hour.'

He instantly rejects the temptation as He did for forty days and nights in the desert before His public ministry began.

> 'No, for this purpose I have come to this hour. Father, glorify Thy Name.....' (*Jn 12.27ff*) 'I have glorified It and I will glorify It again.'

The crowd thought it thundered, others said 'an angel has spoken to Him.'

> 'This Voice is for your sake not for Mine. *Now* is the judgement of this world, now shall the ruler of this world be cast out.' (*Jn 12.28ff*)

The sound of this Voice reminds Him and us of the Baptism, of the Temptation in the desert, and of the Transfiguration. It must prepare His Way, and therefore our response, to the Priestly prayer of *Jn 17.1ff*.

> Father, the hour has come... glorify Thy Son that the Son may glorify Thee... with the glory I had with Thee before the world was made... and I am glorified in them... that they may be one... I in them and Thou in Me that they may be perfectly one so that

the world may know You sent Me... that the Love
You have for Me may be in them, and I in them.
(*Jn 17.1-26*)

From the Beginning, then, 'I am the foundation of your
praying', as He reminds us through Julian of Norwich,
Revelations of Divine Love, chapter 41.*

In the Scriptures, in the lives of the saints, in all of
good-will, we can recognise Christ as Man of Prayer praying for us and with us for others, in loving obedience to
the Father,

Who wills all to be saved. (*Jn 3.17; 12.47*)

Christ's love of the Father in the Holy Spirit makes the
Son's every act more eloquent than all speech because he
is the Word, the one Word necessary for union with God.

I am in the Father and the Father in Me... and we
will make our home with you... the Word which you
hear is not mine but the Father's Who sent Me.
(*Jn 14.10-24*)

---

*   See p. 56 below.

Now is the hour of the Pray-er who is the Word incarnate, who is in the Beginning (*Jn 1.1-5*), eternally present in the now which is for ever; this is the One Voice calling yet always within His and our Incarnational tensions. We can recognise such tensions in:

'I saw Satan fall like lightening...' (*Lk 10.18*)

when he foretells the betrayal of Judas (*Jn 13.21*) and of Peter (*Jn 13.38*); and of myself and each of us.

All the betrayals and countless offences of all time are against His 'first Love' (*I Jn 4.19*) and yet because He loved us first, He made us love-able. Now in the glory of His resurrection He prays for us still as Man of Prayer. So it must be until all is consummated in the Holy Spirit at His Second Coming at the end of time.

We may summarise, for a moment, with a syllogism :

1. Major premise: 'God is Love', *I Jn 4.16.*

2. Minor premise: 'Prayer is love',
   Augustine Baker, OSB, *Holy Wisdom.*

3. Conclusion: Therefore God is Prayer.

Now, therefore, all our hope is in Christ as Man of Prayer, that is, if we can accept that our Redeemer died on the cross. Then we have to see that the worst has already happened. Once the Incomprehensible, the One we call God, has been addressed as 'Father' (*Abba*), by the Man on the cross in His last agony, the resurrection of the Son has to be seen as the only possible *term**, and End of that one Word utterance. It is full, logical, proper to, and Inviolable. It is human in sound, divine in perception but above all, Immortal in Love. We know *now* that Love is stronger than death.

This was what He said throughout His ministry as Man of Prayer. This was why our Lady and His disciples, after His Ascension, were watching and waiting in prayer for the coming of the Holy Spirit. Now, at last, 'in these last days' we see that, in this Spirit of Prayer, the Man of Prayer inspires us within His Body, the Church, 'to listen to Him', 'with the ear of the heart' (*first sentence of the Prologue of the Rule of St Benedict*).

But still 'we doubt and fear' like His disciples on Easter Sunday. We, too, are His incredulous creatures even in our attempts to pray. Simultaneously we touch the credibility gap between us and God and yet because He is also

---

* *Term:* the only possible conclusion. See pp 42, 50, 52 & 105.

Man of Prayer, He draws us into His wonderful compassionate forgiving Love so that we may be One.

> 'Had you not found Me, you could not now be seeking Me.' (*Pascal, Pensées: the Memorial*)

In Him and with Him there can be no such thing as unanswered prayer where prayer is primarily concerned with God rather than need. The point is beautifully illuminated by St John of the Cross asking a Carmelite of Beas,

> 'What does prayer mean to you?'

Madre Francisca de la Madre de Dios replied:

> 'I look upon God's beauty and rejoice that He possesses it.'

Her reply inspired him to compose the last five stanzas of *Esposa* which owes much to his reflections on the *Song of Songs*. Jesus, the Pray-er, in dialogue with the Father shows us what our prayer may be. So, now :

With the drawing of this Love
　　and the Voice of this Calling
　　We shall not cease from exploration
　　And the end of all our exploring
　　Will be to arrive where we started
　　And know the place for the first time

　　………　………　………　………
　　Quick now, here, now, always —
　　A condition of complete simplicity
　　(costing not less than everything)
　　And all shall be well and
　　All manner of thing shall be well
　　When the tongues of flame are in-folded
　　Into the crowned knot of fire
　　And the fire and the rose are one.
　　(from Little Gidding in Four Quartets by TS Eliot)

It is in the prayer-life of Jesus as Man of Prayer more than
in any other activity that we can recognise that He had
to be truly God and truly Man. Through His unique,
infinitely loving, perfected sacrifice our fear of atonement
is transformed by His Priestly prayer :

　　'that they may be one, Father, as we are One'
　　(Jn 17.11ff).

Only through Christ's act of atonement can His human and Divine Heart made One and ever in perfect accord with the Father, give us that heart to Heart at-One-ment we long for.

'Prayer (His-in-us) Oneth the soul to God'
(*Revelations of Divine Love chapter 43*)

So we are moved to pray according to His example and teaching :

Glory be to the Father, and to the Son,
and to the Holy Spirit   —   *Magnificat,*

As It was in the Beginning,
is Now, and ever shall be   —   *Magnificat,*

World without end   —   *Magnificat,*

For the Kingdom, the Power,
and the Glory   —   *Magnificat,*

Are Yours Now and for ever   —   *Magnificat.*

We may accept all that can be said or written about our Lord as Man of Prayer and at the same time feel no personal connection in our attempt to pray. This is where our everyday human feelings can so easily lead us astray. Unless we first look at our Lord as Man of Prayer we withdraw into ourselves. We can then quickly forget that any attempt at prayer for us must always be now, Incarnational and Trinitarian. That means we advert to an already existing personal relationship both fully human and truly divine

'Had you not found Me you could not now be seeking Me.'

It is in this One-ness of heart and mind and purpose alone that we can be fully, rightfully, human and therefore truly ourselves. Always we begin again by first looking at Him because –

In the Son of God, in His blood, we find the redemption that sets us free from our sins. He is the true likeness of the God we cannot see; His is that first birth which precedes every act of creation. Yes, in Him all created things took their being, heavenly and

19

earthly, visible and invisible; what are thrones and dominions, what are princedoms and powers? They were all created through Him and in Him; He takes precedence of all, and in Him all subsist. He too is that head Whose body is the Church; it begins with Him, since His was the first birth out of death; thus in every way the primacy was to become His.

It was God's good pleasure to let all completeness dwell in Him, and through Him to win back all things, whether on earth or in heaven, into Union with Himself, making peace with them through His blood, shed on the Cross. You too, were once estranged from Him; your minds were alienated from Him by a life of sin; but now He has used Christ's natural body to win you back through his death, and so to bring you into His Presence... (*Col 1.15ff*).

If we want to be in His Presence, having first looked to the Pray-er, we must use our gift of common sense in as practical a way as possible. We need a regular approach which might, just might, be set out something like this:

aim at:

regular

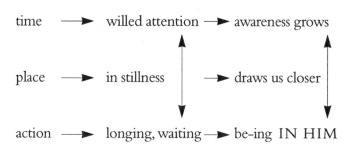

time ⟶ willed attention ⟶ awareness grows

place ⟶ in stillness ⟶ draws us closer

action ⟶ longing, waiting ⟶ be-ing IN HIM

If you prefer something more succinct and to the point:

He is always already there.

Whichever way we read this, or any other technique, no technique, no monomania, can substitute for, nor satisfy, us desiring to be with Him in prayer. Each pray-er is an unique expression of God's Love. Therefore, there is a sense in which the whole of heaven is waiting for my/your next attempt at prayer because only that pray-er can make it. As so often, the psalmist can point the way which our Lord took and turned into His Way:

WHAT IS PRAYER?

'vacate et videte, quoniam ego sum Deus'

'Empty yourself of self to the point of utter stillness and see that I am God'. (*Ps 45.6*)

When He lived this from birth to death, it took Him through Gethsemane to His *kenosis* on the cross (*Phil 2.5*). This can become *now*, in our God-given recognition of the Truth Itself :

'in God alone be at rest my soul' (*Ps 62*),

and

'Father, into your hands I commend My spirit' (*Lk 24.46 & Jn 19.30*).

Despite our faithful attempts at prayer and good works; daily Communion; spiritual reading; and regular confession; spiritual companionship and direction, *etc.*, are we getting anywhere? Do we not feel sometimes that our prayer efforts deserve a more satisfactory reward?

From our limited human point of view this may be so. This may, nonetheless, be a blessing in disguise. Under the pressures of everyday life we easily confuse the God-given desire for perfection which we are born with, and the all too-human demand for perfectibility here and now, according to *my* keen sense of human justice. This may be one of those innumerable moments of grace, when, using our human experience with us and for us, He is giving us, so to speak, a wordless nudge – 'Simon, *Cephas* Peter do stop acting as though it all depends on you, remember, we are in this together.'

In ordinary human terms, when two people talk one must change or there is an *impasse*. What was intended to be a dialogue becomes a monologue, and then a non-relationship. Further communication seems impossible. For the moment, we have forgotten that when we try to pray, to communicate with God, we need first to listen, with the ear of the heart (*St Benedict's Rule, The Prologue*). Then we are already in conversation with Him: unchanging God, change-able man. If we pray for discernment, we may then, with a touch of compunction and an inner smile of relief, recognise our self-block.

It might go something like this:

'Enter into your room and shut the door....and your Father who sees all that is done in secret will reward you. (*Mt 6.6*)

The 'room' is our soul; the willed attention of the listening heart is like a 'sunbeam' or focus of grace; its transitory enlightenment allows us to see what we can only see because the myriad particles of 'dust' (our natural sinful condition) are now temporarily illuminated by a given shaft of 'sun-light'. Then,

> 'in Your light we see light'. (*Ps 35.10*)

and we remember that if we look at the sun, the given natural source of light, it is

> 'dark with excessive bright'. (*Paradise Lost Bk III 380*)

Every attempt at prayer must strengthen our awareness that because of the nature of God,

> 'God is the only central point
> and that Centre is everywhere,'

He cannot be absent to us: we can only be absent to Him by our freely chosen self-imposition. Within this given focus of faith, prayer does not work like a magic wand. It simply allows us to be there in His Presence and then see What is There all the time:

'Something which has existed since the Beginning, that we have heard, and we have seen with our own eyes, that we have watched and touched with our hands: the Word, Who is life – this is our subject.' (*I Jn 1.1*)

Yes, this is our Subject, the Word in the Flesh, Who is Life and Light, Who shines in our darkness. Like Bartimæus, we have to pray,

'Lord, that I may see again'. (*Mk 10.46*)

The infinite Love of God attracts, draws, but never compels us to research 'our subject'. His Love for us is such that unless we wilfully reject Him we know He is always with us whatever our extremity (*Mt 28.20 & Ps 138, The Hound of Heaven*). With the gift of prayer, the following may help us to 'see again' as we try to follow Him along the Way and so see things as He sees them.

First, 'the authentic touch', in the Beginning, as in St John's Prologue (given above *I Jn 1.1ff*). We are then in touch with the ever present, ever new, creative, redemptive Love of God.

Secondly, *echoes*: in His creative *fiat* (see *Genesis 1.3ff*)

'God said let there be light … let there be human beings in our own image and likeness.'

This *fiat* took Flesh in our Lady's *fiat* at the Annunciation. At that moment of her acceptance, the incarnation of the eternal Word, entered into and transcended history (*Lk 1.26ff*). It is re-*present*-ed again by her Son as He takes up the scroll of the prophet Isaiah in the Nazareth Synagogue and looks for the place where it is written:

'this text is being fulfilled today even while you listen'

– with Him it is always *now* (*Lk 4.21*). If we let these and countless other *echoes* of the human and divine speak to us in prayer we will recognise, again and again but as though for the first time, the atoning power of His *fiat* of Gethsemane and the Cross. The 'authentic touch' and the *echo* will remind us of Him through the force of circumstances. Was this not the case with Mary Magdalene? Distraught with grief at finding the tomb empty, and preoccupied with her determination to give him a decent burial, she turned away and would have missed Him had He not called her name. Then she saw, as though for the first time, the feet of the Man she had mistaken for the gardener were pierced (*Jn 20.14*). Later the same day, the two on the road to Emmaus, 'their eyes held' by self-pitying grief – until

they recognised Him in the breaking of the Bread. (*Lk 24.13ff*)

Or the poignancy of Peter's triple affirmation (*Jn 21.15*) echoing and then healing the triple betrayal of Jesus before Caiaphas (*Jn 18.15*).

Thirdly, the gift of a wisdom and discernment which is within but not of this world only. This is recognisable in the five joyful mysteries of the rosary as we prayerfully reflect on what happened at the Annunciation, the Visitation, the Nativity of the Baby, the Presentation of the Child, and the Finding of the Boy in the Temple. Does not this growing awareness of nature and grace working together transform the gift of atonement into at-One-ment, even *now*, as we try to listen in prayer?

Fourthly, the gift of intuition, that is, the immediate arrival at the truth without the otherwise necessary reasoning process. We find a clear example of this in our Lady's directive to the servants at the wedding feast at Cana:

'Do whatever He tells you'

and water became wine (*Jn 2.3ff*). That Mother just knew her Son.

Fifthly, what we may call 'secondary causes'. In my third year in the monastery aged twenty-nine, I met with a sudden unexpected 'accident'. I was attending a Scripture lecture on Charity as found in the letters of St Paul, given by Fr Bruno. He was always late, disorganised and tangent prone. Suddenly he said: 'Well, you know, there are worse things to happen in life than to die...' He had always urged us to call on him if we could not understand or agree. 'This is it', I thought, 'he's asked for it!' I greeted him in his room with, 'How can you be so mad as to say 'There are worse things in life than to die' – what can be worse than death? It's the end of everything!' Startled but dispassionate, he asked 'Have you never heard of the Resurrection?' Full of angry self-justifying frustration, I nearly exploded 'What the hell has that got to do with it?' Mercifully, grace intervened. In the silence that followed his question he began to explain what he believed. My anger drained as he said what the Resurrection meant to him.

When I left his room two hours later, I realised that I had been living without really believing in the Resurrection; that it was the crowning glory of Christ's victory over sin and death, as set out in *I Cor 15*. The way Fr Bruno explained this to me allowed me, incidentally, to see why he was so clearly a good community monk. Reflecting in prayer later, on my outburst and his kindness, I was, after eleven years of self-centred grieving for one I loved beyond description, perhaps beginning to catch a glimpse of what it can mean to live in and with the resurrected Christ – for others.

It is in union with the Man of Prayer, as already suggested, that then the 'authentic touch'; *echoes*; 'wisdom and discernment'; 'intuition', may come together in our attempt at prayer, to help us to become attuned to His grace. I suspect this is especially His Way of helping us interpret 'secondary causes' to His greater glory and our greater happiness. I am sure you have many examples of this within your own experience. It is in this gift of 'interpretation' that we find it easier to forgive one another. His compassion for us must move us to compassion for others in need.

Out of my first real encounter with Fr Bruno developed a mutual affectionate respect. As you know, any gift of grace has to be, in origin, uniquely personal and transparently open to all. He would say during coffee or tea break, 'Come 'n' have a cigarette when you are free.' As a non-smoker, I shared his exhalation as he would begin: 'What do you think of this then? Tell me if you think

I'm mad.' And out would come his latest tangent on scripture, theology, monastic life, and especially people he was trying to help. His concern for others became even clearer during his last ten years after his first heart attack.

Fr Bruno really loved people. He was compassionately understanding of human frailty. I suppose that is why during what turned out to be our last shared 'smoke' he greeted me with an outburst: 'I am unutterably depressed…' He knew, he explained, that he could die at any time, in the next heart attack, but *if only* he could be sure of another ten years he could 'land' those who were floundering and clutching at him for help. 'I'm just beginning to see what it's all about,' he added. I went to remind him of what he'd said about the Resurrection many years ago, but grace intervened; he laughed and asked – 'Did I ever tell you of my worst fear? I dream I shall be on the train somewhere between King's Cross and York trying to get back to Ampleforth when I shall be found dead in the loo; silly isn't it?' Fr Bruno, having received absolution, died on his bed in the monastery, before the doctor arrived 13th August 1967, aged 56. I was away on holiday.

Our attempts to pray with our Lord, Man of Prayer, begin with a one-to-One relationship ('I am the foundation of your praying'). If this is so then we have to go with Him out towards others. We live His '*now*-is-for-ever' not as 'we go it alone', or on a private 'pilgrimage of prayer,' or 'inner life' of our very own, but as we accept we are contingent human beings. Basically it means we are not our own creator. We are utterly dependent on the gift of free air from our first to last moment of life: uniquely individual yet necessarily interdependent. This acceptance takes on a special, infinite, significance when we accept His gifts of Confession and Holy Communion. Then we may grow in awareness of Him in His perfect humanity. We are constantly reminded of this in the daily re-*present*-ation of the one perfect Holy Sacrifice of the Mass. We know that whilst God is not bound by His sacraments they are the normal channels of grace guaranteeing the truth of His

'I am with you always, even until the end of time'. (*Mt 28.20*)

The Sacrament of Confession or Reconciliation calls us back to where we really want to be – at peace with Him and one another. If we look at Him *first* we are already making the act of faith-and-prayer-in-One of Bartimæus:

'Lord, let me see again'. (*Mt 10.51*)

31

With our spiritual sight restored we recognise, once again, and as though for the first time, that Christ's gift of reconciliation, alone, makes us fully human and truly ourselves.

After first sharing his prayer of at-One-ment we will be ready to see our sins as He sees them, symptoms of a dis-ease crying out for healing, for whole-ness, for holi-ness. Then touched by this insight, we recognise that any thought, word, deed, or omission, not a reflection of His humanity, makes us that degree less human. It is our natural susceptibility to sin, if unchecked, that begins a softening up process towards a disintegration of person-al responsibility; self-alienation; and a loss of personal integrity. This must have a knock-on effect on others.

In some such on-going, growing, spiritual awareness we experience that we cannot be completely ourselves without Him and in Him for others. We see again: He made us; He redeemed us; He calls us back; and so He must forgive us because His Love is unconditional – if we will accept It. Then we become again fully ourselves because we are once again fully in accord with Him in His and only perfect humanity.

It is now that a properly informed conscience opens us to His gift of Peace:

'Conscience is that inner living sense which tells me what I ought to do. As a Christian it tells me what I am and what I ought to be.'

Calmly, in His presence, we are now ready, free from fear and anxiety, for an honest to God examination of conscience.

We might, as an example, take what St Thomas Aquinas calls the 'Compassion of God'.

First, God never reproaches anyone for natural defects be they *bodily defects e.g.*, blindness, deafness, lameness; or any other deformity. Nor does He reproach us for *mental handicaps* such as limited understanding, seeming stupidity, lack of memory or reason, or discernment.

Secondly, God is severely reproachful of *spiritual defects* which with grace can be overcome *e.g.*, ingratitude for His gifts, desire for superfluities, resentment at the success of the just, or joy at their affliction; or the belittling or blackening the good of another; or any apathy for goodness.

Thirdly, He reproaches self-love, self-opinion; keenness to win favour of others; our hatred of correction, our love of praise, our self-pity, seeking consolations, our self-indulgence; or our carnal affections and desires.

Therefore, St Thomas concludes: despise no one for

lacking health, bodily integrity, energy, good looks, eloquence, or the lack of any other gift. Rather be ready to praise God for His gifts to others and try to supply all their defects.

Thirteenth century St Thomas in his 'Compassion of God' *echoes* the spirit of sixth century *St Benedict's Rule, chapter 72: On the Good Zeal of Monks* which begins:

> Just as there is a wicked zeal of bitterness which separates from God and leads to hell, so there is a good zeal which separates from evil and leads to God and everlasting life...

Surely, together, and with any other examples we may recall, do they not in their 'authentic touch' *echo* the story of the 'Prodigal's Father' (*Lk 15.20ff*)? As we listen to the words of His absolution:

> I absolve you from your sins
> in the Name of the Father and of the Son
> and of the Holy Spirit

making the sign of the Cross, we take them to heart. We know we are forgiven. It is the nature of His extraordinary Love that He loves the repentant sinner even more than ever. All four gospels and the teaching of His Church proclaim this truth. The Petrine text, the 'power of the keys' (*Mt 16.16ff*) is confirmed at His Ascension:

> All authority in heaven and on earth has been given to me... Go, therefore to all peoples... (*Mt 28.18ff*)

It is clear that His gift of Baptism is for the forgiveness of sins; that His gift of atonement is for our at-One-ment, now and for ever. In this life we need His Sacrament of return and renewal, so that our heart may remain open to the promptings of the Holy Spirit. This is what the 'Compassion of God' constantly keeps alive within us: we are fallen, but redeemed.

> I have fallen but shall rise again, though I dwell in darkness the Lord God is my Light. (*Micah 7.8*)

This is why we pray,

> Lord, I believe, help my unbelief. (*Mk 9.25*)

then we see why and how the Spirit of repentance and contrition prepares us for the reception of Holy Communion:

> Though we are sinners,
> we trust in Your mercy and love.
> Do not consider what we truly deserve,
> but grant us Your forgiveness.
> (*Eucharistic Prayer I, prayer for us sinners*)

It is right and fitting therefore that the daily sacrifice of the Mass begins with an act of contrition.

It is, then, in this Spirit that we must make our Holy Communion, our One-ing with Him

So that all may be One (*Jn 17.21ff*)

as we eat His Body and drink His Blood (see *The Catechism of the Catholic Church 1994, pp. 299ff*). This is our spiritual food and drink for everlasting life (*Jn 6.50ff*).

The shocking intimacy of this act of faith-and-prayer-in-One is re-*present*-ed in every Mass throughout the world daily. Within the Mass we are reminded, and enter again, but as though for the first time, into His redeeming, atoning life, death and resurrection as we become One with Him. As we pray the Mass, in such a Real intimacy, we share one state of *be*-ing for the living and the dead.

This Infinite Truth has to be conveyed to us by a kind

of divine shorthand of signs and symbols. For example, the bread and wine presented at the offertory: then re-*present*-ed after the consecration. They look, feel, smell and taste the same both before and after the consecration. But the words of consecration are His, using the hands and voice of His priest. Only His Word, the living-in-the-flesh-Word, Resurrected, and so glorified, speaks the difference (*cf Lauda Sion, Adoro Te, O Bread of Heaven, etc.*).

Listening with faith and Love, we are then ready to respond, as fully as His infinite grace allows, to the words:

'the Body of Christ' *and* 'the Blood of Christ'.

We reply:

'Amen – so be It – yes, with all my heart'
– 'in Him, with Him'

– for others. He said at the Last Supper:

I am the vine… (*Jn 15. 1ff*)

Cut off from Him we die: we are His contingent beings. The power and beauty of this Image is full of grace even as the gift of our focus in prayer: let vine become vein and His Blood becomes our Life-blood: One main life-line of Communication in time, for eternity, *now*, and for ever.

Just as we believe (because God wills all to be saved) in the Church's teaching on the Baptism of desire; so may we offer Mass and Communion for those in need – for the sick, the suffering; for the dis-eased in heart or mind; for the handicapped; lonely, wavering, 'lost' yet still search-ing; for the most seemingly hardened, abandoned, 'fail-ure'; for, and with, those who have died. No accident in life or death, unless freely chosen, can block His infinite Mercy. The 'Compassion of God' transcends the limita-tions of our finite logic and thinking. This must be espe-cially so in anything that inhibits or handicaps the freedom of choice at the moment of death. As we enter into *this* Mass and *this* Communion with our Lord, Man of Prayer, He, the Pray-er in His Eucharistic act of perfect Love, remembers with us

> Those for whom we offer this sacrifice,
> especially *N. & N...*
> and all the dead
> whose faith is known to You alone.
> (*cf. Eucharistic Prayers I-IV*)

At the breaking of the Bread, His body and the pouring out of the Wine, His blood,

> we come to share in the divinity of Christ
> Who humbled Himself to share in our humanity.

So, we share by His incarnation One Life-giving vein of a Whole common-Unity which is the Holiness of His Real Presence* at-One-with-us in Love.

Before first communicating, the priest prays silently:

> Lord Jesus Christ,
> with faith in Your Love and Mercy,
> I eat Your Body and drink Your Blood.
> Let It not bring me condemnation
> but healing in mind and body.

Alternatively,

> Lord Jesus Christ, Son of the Living God,
> by the will of the Father

---

* *cf The Catechism of the Catholic Church 1994, pp. 309-10 and pp. 318-9* for a brief, clear exposition of the traditional teaching about this most special and unique reflection of Christ's presence.

and the work of the Holy Spirit,
Your death brought Life to the world.
By Your holy Body and Blood
free me from all my sins and from every evil.
Keep me faithful to Your teaching,
and never let me be parted from You.

If we experience, alone and together, a wordless stillness after our Communion, we know…

       there is no vocabulary
For Love within a family, love that's lived in
But not looked at, love within the light of which
All else is seen, the love within which
All other love finds speech.
This Love is silent.
(from The Elder Statesman by TS Eliot)

This is the dynamic silent Love of the Real Presence at
the heart-core of the Mass, which is the Heart of the
Body of Christ, which is His Church.

This is why we read in *chapter III §13* of the Vatican II
decree *On the Ministry and Life of Priests*:

They are strongly urged to celebrate daily, for even if

the faithful cannot be present this is an act of Christ and of the Church. Thus priests offer themselves wholly to God each day as they unite themselves with the priestly action of Christ, and in being nourished by the body of Christ they fill their hearts with the love of him who gives himself as food for the faithful.

We meet this privileged, daily obligation to pray with Him and in Him for others, also in what we call the Divine Office. In *The Constitution on the Sacred Liturgy, chapter IV §83ff*, it reminds us that:

> Jesus Christ, High Priest of the New and Eternal Covenant, taking human nature, introduced into this earthly exile that hymn which is sung throughout all ages... He continues His priestly work through His Church... by celebrating the Eucharist... and the divine office... which is the very prayer of Christ... within His Body, the Church, addresses to the Father.*

Our every effort to pray, individually and collectively, privately and publicly, must be founded on an objective truth

---

* See also *The Introduction to The Divine Office according to the Roman Rite*, and *The General Instruction on the Liturgy of the Hours*.

of dogma and require our subjective acceptance, *e.g.*,

> God is Love and anyone who lives in love lives in God,
> and God lives in him… (*I Jn 4.16ff*)

So, Tertullian, an early Christian commentator (born AD 150) begins his treatise on the Resurrection with '*caro cardo salutis*', 'the flesh is the door-hinge of salvation' simply because the Incarnation must lead us to the Resurrection. The Truth is that 'the Redeemer in the womb', the 'Word made Flesh' must come to full *term** as the resurrected and glorified Christ (*Jn 1.1ff*). But what about us? What about *my* resurrection? Tertullian replies:

> It will be easier for you to be made once more what
> you have already been, in that equally without diffi-
> culty you have been made what once you never were.

Yes, but… if only… the 'authentic touch', the *echoes*, the 'secondary causes'? Have you never heard of the Resurrection?

If Christ has not been raised, you are still in your sins.

---

* See *pp. 15, 50, 52 & 105*.

And what is more serious, all who have died in Christ have perished. If our hope in Christ has been for this life only, we are the most unfortunate of all people… someone may ask, 'How are dead people raised, and what sort of body do they have when they come back?' They are stupid questions.

Whatever you sow in the ground has to die before it is given new life; and the thing that you sow is not what is going to come; you sow a bare grain, say of wheat or something like that, and then God gives it the sort of body that He has chosen; each sort of seed gets its own sort of body… when this perishable nature has put on imperishability, and when this mortal nature has put on immortality, then the words of scripture will come true: 'Death is swallowed up in victory. Death, where is your victory? Death, where is your sting?' Now the sting of death is sin and sin gets its power from the Law. So let us thank God for giving us the victory through our Lord Jesus Christ. Never give in then, my dear brothers and sisters, never admit defeat; keep on working at the Lord's work always, knowing that, in the Lord, you cannot be labouring in vain. (*I Cor 15. 17-19, 35-38, 54-58*)

Do *you* believe this?

Yes, Lord, I believe: help my unbelief. (*Mk 9.25*)

Yes, I am compelled to believe in the resurrection of the body and everlasting life for five reasons.

1. The first, because of what I call 'Man's Malice'. This is the largest and most negative area of consideration.

2. Secondly, I am compelled to believe in the resurrection of the body and everlasting life because of 'God's Love.'

3. Thirdly, because of what I call 'Epiphany' or the showing forth of the Divine in human terms.

4. Fourthly, I am compelled to believe in the resurrection of the body and everlasting life because of His gift of 'Reconciliation'.

5. Fifthly, because of one single short statement: Love is stronger than death.

So let us consider these five points more fully :

1. Man's malice:

malice   = active ill-will,
then as *now*.

contemporary reporting = then as *now*, by word of
mouth later written up.

First, I am compelled to believe in 'the resurrection of
the body and the life everlasting' (*Apostles' Creed*)
because the Jewish leaders were too determined to
discredit it. Those full-time theocrats who claimed
to be best instructed to know better, seem motivat-
ed by malice and fear. The accounts that come to
us from the Scriptures and contemporary reporting
reveal this. Witness their decision to murder Lazarus
because 'that imposter, the carpenter's son' had raised
Lazarus from the dead and, as a result of that, the people were leaving them and following 'this Jesus of
Nazareth': *cf Jn 11.49ff & 12.11* and such extant frag-
ments of contemporary reporting as may be found in
the Jewish 'historian' Josephus who died in AD 93;
Roman Pliny who died in AD 110, and Roman
Tacitus who died in AD 116; and, as already men-
tioned the Christian, Tertullian born in AD 150.
There can be no doubt about the historical existence

and public crucifixion of a man called Jesus of Nazareth.

The rigidity and fear of the Jewish leaders and the anti-reporters strikes a chord in me. In it all I recognise that determination to find any and every excuse to prove wrong what I do not want to believe. They had seen 'his power' over life and death in others, and the effect of it upon others, especially amongst ordinary people longing for a better way of life, for goodness, for God: *cf* the raising of Jairus's daughter (*Mt 9.15; Mk 5.41; Lk 8.55*) and the widow of Nain's only son (*Lk 7.11*). The professional theocrats dared not risk the now possibility of a 'self resurrection'. This 'madness' had to be stopped. There was too much at stake that would be too humiliating for such professionals to face. Therefore they stressed 'his' death. They, not the Romans, feared his 'resurrection'. They begged Pilate to have the tomb sealed and guarded for three days. You have your guards, he said, you see to it (*cf Mt 27.65ff*). They did; and so did the Romans – guards watching the guards – no risk of any tricks there then.

Then on the third day... they handed a considerable sum of money to the soldiers with these instructions – you are to say, 'His disciples came during the night and stole him away while we were asleep.' (*Mt 28.13*)

The soldiers took the money and passed on the message, of course. But what self-respecting soldier would go around saying 'whilst we were asleep on guard duty'? And if they were asleep how did they know what happened? With what 'nod and a wink' did they spread it around? 'And to this day...' as we know, best -seller paper-backs tell how 'he' only seemed to die; 'he' was drugged and revived by his followers. And having recovered 'he' went off with Mary Magdalene. They do say you 'believe what you want to believe'.

None of this, not even all of it, moves me so much as the silent witness of a second century block of stone, excavated at the end of the nineteenth century from the ruins of the Palatine Palace and now in the National Museum in Rome. Scratched on it there is a blasphemous cartoon *shewing* the crucifixion of a man with an ass's head. The head is looking down, left, to a man who stands looking up at it. Underneath, in Greek, are scratched the words '*ΑΛΕΞΑΜΕΝΟΣ ΧΕΒΕΤΕ ΘΕΟΝ*': 'Alexamenos adores his god.' A later hand added in Latin,

'*Alexamenos fidelis*', 'Alexamenos was faithful' (understood) 'even unto death, even death on a cross.'

This blasphemy is the earliest extant depicture of Christ's crucifixion. Alexamenos, thought to be a convert Greek slave, died during one of the worst second century waves of persecution in the early Church. At the time and probably into the fifth century, Christians could not bear to look upon any thing showing Christ naked on the cross. And prudence, at least, would suggest that it would be foolish to display any Christian sign of the cross until some time after Constantine's conversion in the fourth century.

2. **God's Love:**

Please see page 2 and then note: we know the Love of God in Itself cannot be put into words; we can come to recognise and experience that His Love is

The one thing necessary (*Lk 10.42*)

but not apart from Him. If we put ourselves outside this relationship we slide into erroneous thinking and hardening of heart. See the section on 'Man's Malice' above, page 45.

'Discredited your own thinking': Caiaphas distorted the messianic prophecy to save face (*Jn 11.50*); Pilate having pronounced the Prisoner 'a just man' washed his hands 'of the blood of this innocent man' when his career was endangered: *cf Mt 27.25; Mk 15.10; Lk 23.20; Jn 18.28.* Pilate's

Truth, what is that? (*Jn 18.38*)

haunts us still as we try to distinguish the true from the false; or face a dilemma; or a crisis of conscience. The worst has already happened.

Thus we recognise when grace allows us to see that in Christ's death, freely accepted, sin and death have been over-powered by God's Love: *cf Revelations of Divine Love, chapter 22.*

Secondly, then, it is above all that God's love compels me to 'believe in the resurrection of the body and the life everlasting' because once His death is accepted no greater test of credibility is possible. If you can think of a worse or a greater act of malice than man's determination to try to kill God you have discredited your own thinking – like the Jewish leaders, or poor Pilate – but if, if you can accept that our Redeemer died on the cross, then we have to see the worst has already happened. Once the Incomprehensible, the One we call God, has been addressed as 'Father' by the Man on the cross in His last agony, the Resurrection of the Son has to be seen as the only possible *term** of that utterance. It is full, logical, proper (belonging to), and Inviolable. It is human in sound, divine in perception, but above all Immortal in Love.

3. Epiphany:
(the showing forth of the divine in human terms)

Thirdly, I am compelled to 'believe in the resurrection of the body and the life everlasting' because of His appearances after the Resurrection as they come to me through the Scriptures and the living tradition of the Church; and in, especially, the daily re-*present*ation of His Real Presence under the appearances of bread and wine; and within the witness of the lives of the saints, that is, of all those who try to live in and with the risen Christ where nothing lasts – except the truth Itself.

---

*   See *pp. 15, 42, 52 & 105.*

4. Reconciliation:
(if necessary please refer back to page 31)

Fourthly, I am compelled to 'believe in the resurrection of the body and the life everlasting' because I have experienced, and continue to hope for, His forgiveness through life as it comes to me in His sacrament of Confession; and within my Community's forgiveness of me; and all I offend, for all my countless failings where I recognise that it is human to err but divine to forgive. You show me the way as He did before, and especially in His last agony on the cross when He said:

> Father, forgive them for they know not what they do (*Lk 23.34*)

and in His reply to the repentant thief,

> Indeed I promise you, this day you will be with Me in paradise. (*Lk 23.43*)

5. Love *is* stronger than death:
(simply, because such is my experience)

Fifthly, Christ has risen, therefore 'in my End is my Beginning'. 'With the drawing of this Love and the Voice of this Calling' (see page 17) we enter into Christ's confrontation with everything alien to the Spirit. With Him, in our attempts at prayer, we are *now*, and for ever, His Easter people. We pray with Him, *now* in His Christophony, that is, we live and die with Him in His Resurrection as He teaches us by word and sacrament in His Body, the Church.

With our Lady, St Peter, the apostles and all the saints we are awaiting His Christophany, that is, the manifestation of His Second Coming at the last day. Then, with them, and all of good-will, we shall recognise, in the End, the full *term** of the Second Person of the Trinity (as though for the first time) in the One fullness of human and divine *be*-ing. Then, within Him and this great throng of witnesses (*Hebrews 12. 1ff*), we shall be transformed in Christ's love for us and for the Father. This is perfectly expressed by St John of the Cross (from *Songs of the soul in rapture*):

> *Amado con amada*
> *Amada en el Amado transformada.*

---

* See *pp. 15, 42, 50 & 105.*

'*Amado con amada...*' might be paraphrased: 'When Christ the Lover of souls looks upon a soul with his love, that soul, in a state of grace, is so drawn to Him that each is transfigured into the other.' Whilst this state of perfect at-One-ment is possible here and now, it is not yet the fullness of the Beatific Vision (*cf p. 71*).

The following twelve quotations, with tentative notes, may illustrate, better than I dare hope, the on-going attempt to answer *What is Prayer?* Until the end of time it must remain an open-ended question. As we try to respond to His call for at-One-ment we may experience a poignant incommunicable sadness and joy:

> Late have I loved Thee,
> O Beauty so ancient and so new;
> late have I loved Thee.
> (*Confessions of St Augustine, Book X.27*)

1. The 'Theology'* of Prayer of Julian of Norwich

REVELATIONS OF DIVINE LOVE
by Julian of Norwich

Julian was not a Scripture or theology scholar. Yet the written account of the Revelations of Divine Love contains an orthodox familiarity with both Scripture and theology approved by the Church. Scholars of every or no demonination today applaud the soundness of her well informed grace-filled intuitions. What is now available has stood the test of time. It appeals to an ever-widening public. If you read slowly and reflectively the five extracts you will be free to respond to and so recognise for yourself that they present one complete statement of what prayer is and, so to speak, how it works. See also pp. 69*ff* and pp. 89*ff.*

This introduction to Julian's 'theology' of prayer will lead us to an awareness that whatever we may 'see' in prayer must draw us as nothing else can. This is simply because 'Love is the only answer' to all our best desires. What would you add to this?

---

* For an explanation of this term, see Introduction, as above.

A. Chapter 6

To know the goodness of God is the highest prayer of all, and it is a prayer that accommodates itself to our most lowly needs. It quickens our soul, and vitalises it, developing it in grace and virtue. Here is the grace most appropriate to our needs, and most ready to help. Here is the grace which our soul is seeking now, and which it will ever seek until that day when we know for a fact that he has wholly united us to himself. He does not despise the work of his hands, nor does he disdain to serve us, however lowly our natural need may be. He loves the soul he has made in his own likeness.

For just as the body is clothed in its garments, and the flesh in its skin, and the bones in their flesh, and the heart in its body, so too are we, soul and body, clothed from head to foot in the goodness of God. Yes, and even more closely than that for all these things will decay and wear out, whereas the goodness of God is unchanging, and incomparably more suited to us. Our lover desires indeed that our soul should cleave to him with all its might, and ever hold on to his goodness. Beyond our power to imagine does this most please God and speed the soul on its course.

The love of God Most High for our soul is so

wonderful that it surpasses all knowledge. No created being can know the greatness, the sweetness, the tenderness of the love that our Maker has for us. By his grace and help therefore let us in spirit stand and gaze, eternally marvelling at the supreme, surpassing, single-minded, incalculable love that God, who is goodness, has for us. Then we can ask reverently of our lover whatever we will. For by nature our will wants God, and the good will of God wants us. We shall never cease wanting and longing until we possess him in fulness and joy. Then we shall have no further wants. Meanwhile his will is that we go on knowing and loving until we are perfected in heaven.

B. *Chapter 41*

I now see that there are two conditions about prayer. One concerns its rightness, the other our sure trust.

Often enough our trust is not wholehearted, for we are not sure that God hears us. We think it is due to our unworthiness and because we feel absolutely nothing: we are often as barren and dry after our prayers as we were before. This awareness of our foolishness is the cause of our weakness. At least, this has been my own experience.

All this our Lord brought immediately to mind, and in this revelation said, 'I am the foundation of your praying. In the first place my will is that you should pray, and then I make it your will too, and since it is I who make you pray, and you do so pray, how can you not have what you ask for?'

C. Chapter 42

Sometimes it seems to us that we have been praying a long time, and yet we do not see any answer. We should not get despondent because of this. I believe our Lord intends by this either that we should await a more suitable time, or more grace, or a better gift. He wills that we should have true knowledge of himself that he is all-being: our understanding must be rooted in the knowledge, as strongly, deliberately and sincerely as we are able to make it. Here we are to stand and stay. By his own gracious light he wants us to understand the following things: (i) the distinction and excellence of our creation, (ii) the price and value of our redemption, and (iii) everything created has been put under us to serve us, and is upheld by him out of love for us. This is his meaning, as if to say, 'See, I have done all this long before your prayers; and now you exist, and pray to me.' He means that we ought to

57

know that the greatest deeds are already done, as Holy Church teaches. Gratefully realising this we ought to be praying for the deed *now* in process, which is that he should rule and guide us in this life for his own glory, and bring us to his bliss.

D. Chapter 43

Prayer unites the soul to God. However like God the soul may be in essence and nature (once it has been restored by grace), it is often unlike him, in fact, because of man's sin. Then it is that prayer proclaims that the soul should will what God wills; and it strengthens the conscience and enables a man to obtain grace. God teaches us to pray thus, and to trust firmly that we shall have what we ask. For he looks at us in love, and would have us share in his good work. So he moves us to pray for what it is he wants to do. For such prayer and good will – and it is his gift – he rewards us eternally. And the word 'and you do so pray' shows all this. In it God takes as great pleasure and delight as if he were indebted to us for all the good we do. And yet it is he who actually does it! Because we pray earnestly that he should do whatever he wills, it is as though he said, 'What can please me more than to have you pray fervently, wisely, and earnestly to do what I am going to do?' So does the soul by prayer conform to God.

E. *Chapter 5*

God showed me too the pleasure it gives him when a simple soul comes to him, openly, sincerely and genuinely. It seems to me as I ponder this revelation that when the Holy Spirit touches the soul it longs for God rather like this: 'God, of your goodness give me yourself, for you are sufficient for me. I cannot properly ask anything less, to be worthy of you. If I were to ask less, I should always be in want. In you alone do I have all.'

2. Examples from the 1st to the 20th centuries

A. *Example I*

One thing is necessary – the love of God
(*Lk 10.42*)

because

In the beginning was the Word… (*Jn 1.1ff*)

and because

God loved us first

and therefore because

> God is love, they who live in love live in God
> and He lives in them. (*I Jn 4.10ff*)

Comment

This is why, even in this life, though we cannot know God directly and live, we can experience Him in love directly, or at least as we may recognise Him in the 'authentic touch' or *echo*.

At Bethany, Mary Magdalene was drawn into the prayer of the listening heart (*Lk 10.42*). She then recognised Him at last, and as though for the first time, as the Word dwelling amongst us: the Love of God Incarnate. She had met Him before but in this Heart to heart she was simply impervious to all else. In this Presence, *now*, she knew the Love of God to be the 'One thing necessary.' Such a sublime Necessity enabled her to watch Him die on the Cross; and then, 'on the third day' find Him alive, after she had mistaken Him for the gardener (*Jn 20.15*).

B. Example II: First Century

> Something which has existed
> since the beginning
> that we have heard
> and we have seen with our own eyes,
> that we have watched
> and touched with our own hands:
> the Word, Who is life —
> this is our Subject.

Comment

In this ambience of Gospel faith, the Love of God for all of good-will is ever present (*cf Jn 1. 1ff; Jn 13-17; Ps 45.6; Ps 62*). Often contrary to outward appearances, the Love of God speaks, always *now*, to the human heart and community in multifarious ways. St Luke's 'One thing' becomes St John's 'Something', recognisable then, and for ever, as One and the Self-same 'Subject'. Recognised by Luke, John, and Mary Magdalene, and *now* by us, he is, both before and after the Resurrection, necessarily the same Person. Truly recognised and named by St John:

'It is the Lord, Who is Life — this is our Subject. (*Jn 21.7*)

Any prayerful intervention, His and ours, of this Subject is the 'Gospel vein' of all the following quotations. They invoke a fulfilment of life possible only within a rapport (personal and communal) with the Spirit of our Lord, Ascended Man of Prayer.

C. Example III: Fourth Century

You have created us and redeemed us and You therefore draw us to Yourself. So our heart finds no peace until it rests in You.
(*Confessions of St Augustine 1.1*)

Comment

Three centuries on, St Augustine witnesses to the Ascended Man of Prayer both by his experience and teaching. The praying-faith of his 'Confessions' proclaims his conviction that 'our heart finds no peace until it rests in You', even whilst his heart cries out, 'Late have I loved You, O Beauty, so Ancient and so New, late have I loved You.'

In a life's struggle, St Augustine learned to accept that the Truth alone gives Continence where an unconditional surrender, in Love, releases that compunction of heart which merging into one Heart-to-heart, gives a peace the world cannot give. Such a gift comes within One integrity which must be both human and divine.

It was this faith that enabled him to continue, as Bishop of Hippo, to carry on writing up his vision of *The City of God* even whilst the Barbarians were battering down the city gates.

D. Example IV: Sixth Century

God says to you: if you will have true and everlasting life, keep your tongue from evil and your lips that they speak no guile. Turn away from evil and do good: seek after peace and pursue it (*Ps 33.4 & I Peter 3.10*). And when you have done these things, my eyes will be upon you and my ears open to your prayers. And before you call upon Me (*cf Is 58.9*) I shall say to you, 'Lo, here I AM'. (*Ex 3.13; Jn 8.58; 18.5*). What can be sweeter to us than the voice of our Lord inviting us? Behold in His loving mercy the Lord shows us the way of life. (*Prologue of the Rule of St Benedict*)

Comment

The 'one thing necessary' (*Lk 10.42*) – the Love of God – makes St Benedict's life and *Rule* integral. This was so in his life-time as it is today. Known as 'man of God, man of prayer', his integrity of heart and mind and purpose allowed him to discern, and speak directly to, the listening heart. This gave him a teaching authority which appeals for, but does not pre-empt, the need for a decision – 'God says to you: if you will…' and then the prerequisites for honest to God prayer follow.

Looking to God first, His gift of freedom of choice being properly informed, the pray-er sees again: 'in His loving mercy the Lord shows us the way of life'. Does this not, then and *now*, resonate for us the One-to-one relationship within the *familia** of Bethany; the Last Supper; and, God help us, the Cross? Not, you notice, 'I tell you… do this… don't do that' but 'God says to you: if you will…' then we know that 'before you call upon Me… *now* – here I AM.'

'If you will… truly seek God' with quiet joy, then

---

* *familia*: family to be interpreted literally in its human and divine most personal particular sense and in its widest most comprehensive sense. That is, my family or your family; the human family; the Holy family of the Our Father now one in nature and grace. In this prayer of his at-One-ment everything is 'familiar' in the best sense of the Word, *cf* the family of One communion (pp. 36*ff*) and TS Eliot's *Family Reunion*. Then, if you will, look forward to being at home within one Holy Family (pp. 67, 85 & 112).

St Benedict re-*present*-s Christ's life of at-One-ment, through listening-obedience to the Father. This must always be the Spirit of the gospels and the *Rule*. We may experience His 'authentic touch' in this quotation from St Benedict's *Prologue to the Rule* as it *echoes* the Scriptures. And with a shared 'intuition' the texts can reverberate for us again and again the Original inspiration, namely :

1. 'Turn away from evil and do good, seek after peace and pursue it,' from *Ps 33.4*, recited by our Lord, Man of Prayer, on the Cross. After the resurrection – and his triple affirmation – St Peter, healed by compunction of heart, can help others to repent (*I Pet 3.10*). By reiterating this psalm for us and with us, St Benedict (and St Peter) leads us back to the Original, 'if you will… take up your Cross and follow Me' (*Lk 9.23*).

2. 'Before you call upon Me…' echoing *Is 58.9* – 'You will call and he will say I AM here.'

3. 'I AM' echoing *Ex 3.13* by way of *Jn 8.58* – 'before Abraham was I AM'; and in Gethsemane, the 'I AM He' of *Jn 18.5*.

In this, and countless other examples, always 'the text is being fulfilled today even as we listen' (*Lk 4.21*) and long to respond. No text however close to the Truth (I am the Way, the Truth and the Life: *Jn 14.6*) will motivate us for long if we do not take it into an undivided heart and act upon it. Witness the mood swings of the Nazara Synagogue congregation. From spontaneous praise of Him one moment to trying to kill Him the next for His teaching on the same text (*Lk 4.28*). And the two attempts to murder St Benedict (see the *Dialogues of St Gregory the Great*).

'Listen' is the first word of the *Prologue to St Benedict's Rule*. Listen attentively 'with the ear of your heart', after that, 'if you will...' occurs six times in the

---

* St Gregory, the first Benedictine Pope, in his very brief *Life*, tells how St Benedict became Abbot of neighbouring monks clamouring for reform. Envious of his holiness they were incapable of following his exemplary life. They put poison in the wine. St Benedict blessed it; its container shattered; the plot was revealed; he returned to his cave in Subiaco.

Next, Florentius, a priest, jealous of St Benedict's high standing with the local people, sent him a poisoned loaf as a sign of Christian fellowship. Again, the plot was revealed by divine intuition; and St Benedict left for Monte Cassino where he was to write his *Rule*. Details of these murderous machinations can be found in *chapters III & VIII* of St Gregory the Great's *St Benedict*.

Prologue. As Abbot, the loving father of a spiritual, supposedly adult, family, St Benedict knew from hard experience you cannot dictate to the heart. Only the now familiar prayer of at-One-ment gives lasting stability to true family life whether natural or spiritual.

E. *Example V: Twelfth Century*

Sometimes, Lord You send into my heart a something *I know not what.* I experience a savour so sweet and comforting that were it fulfilled in me I would seek nothing more. You do not permit me to learn what *it* is: by no vision of the eye, or feeling, or understanding. I would hold it fast and savour it, but it passes swiftly. *Whatever it be,* I accept it, hoping that it will profit me to eternal life. But would that I could keep it longer, and transmit its power into the veins and marrow of my soul, so that *all lower love might die* in me. (*De contemplando Deo,* William of St Thierry)

Comment

In this quotation we encounter the longing and waiting of a truly humble loving pray-er. Poised to respond in utter simplicity he confesses: 'Sometimes, Lord, you send into my heart a *Something, I know not what* – would I could transmit It into the veins and marrow of my soul so that all lower love might die in me'.

This is not the 'angst' or death wish of a Romantic lover. It is the received, handed on Truth, *de contemplando Deo*, as experienced by a man of prayer, who was incidentally, an excellent theologian, scripture and patristic scholar. William, of Saint-Thierry, near Rheims, was elected Abbot aged about thirty-four in 1119. He resigned after sixteen years. Seeking a more clearly defined solitude and silence, in order to draw closer to God, he joined the Benedictine Cistercian reformers at Signy. Soon he became a confessor to neighbouring Carthusians. He wrote for their and our (and his own?) encouragement, his famous *Golden Epistle*. It contains within three lines, the ever-present prophetic *echo*

cum quo enim Deus est	he with whom God is
numquam minus solus est	is never less alone
quam cum solus est	than when he is alone.

Can we *now* rate his solemn perpetual vows of Stability and *Conversatio Morum* and Obedience? 'I steady as a water in a well, to a poise, to a pane' (pane of glass –

an image of absolute pure transparent Stillness)... 'Of the Gospel proffer, a pressure, a principle, a Christ's gift' (from *The Wreck of the Deutschland, stanza 4, GM Hopkins SJ*). Again and again we may recognise *echoes* from the earliest times:

Be still, and see that I am God. (*Ps 45.6*)

In God alone be at rest my soul. (*Pss 61.1 & 62*)

F *Example VI: Fourteenth Century*
God, of your goodness give me yourself, for you are sufficient for me. I cannot properly ask anything less, to be worthy of you. If I were to ask less, I should always be in want. *In you alone do I have all.* (*Revelations of Divine Love, chapter 5, Julian of Norwich*)

Comment
We have already met Julian of Norwich as woman of prayer in her *Revelations of Divine Love* (pp. 55-9). We cannot, as yet, thank her adequately for sharing His *shewings.* At least let us, *now*-and-on-the-Way, seek One-ness in prayer in the Spirit of her conclusions:

So it was that I learned that love was our Lord's

meaning... before ever he made us, God loved us... In his Love all his works have been done, and in this love he has made everything serve us; and in this love our life is everlasting. Our beginning was when we were made, but the love in which he made us never had beginnings. In It we have our beginning. All this we shall see in God for ever. May Jesus grant this. Amen.' (*Revelations of Divine Love p. 212*)

A fuller commentary follows later; see pages 89*ff.*

G. *Example VII: Fourteenth Century*

That which I am, I offer to you, O Lord, for *You are it entirely.* (*Book of Privy Counselling, chapter I*)

Whatever we may say of it is not *it,* but only about it. (*Book of Privy Counselling, chapter XI*)

Comment

If we add these quotations from the *Book of Privy Counselling* to our later references (pages 95*ff*) to the *Cloud of Unknowing* we may, 'if you will', meet the anonymous author, personally.

Persevering in prayer with the Ascended Man of

Prayer we shall find ourselves drawn to the Centre of all true spiritual affinity '....then we shall be seeing face to face (*I Cor 13.12ff*) where there can be, 'my dear friend', no anonymity... then I shall know just as fully as I am myself known.'

H. Example VIII: Sixteenth Century

Give me at once Thyself; send me no more a messenger who cannot tell me what I wish...
(*Song between Soul and Bridegroom*)

O Darkness lovelier than the dawn
(*Divine Poems: Song of Soul in Rapture*)

...in depthless caverns of awareness
(*Living Flame of Love*)

Comment

St John of the Cross is sometimes presented either as a lesser St Teresa or a depersonalised doctoral thesis of inhuman perfection. Surely there has to be laughter in heaven! His sketch of the ascent of Mount Carmel (p. 72) was placed at the beginning of the *Ascent*. It is a summary of the teaching contained in that book. The paradox of his teaching *echoes* that of the gospels.

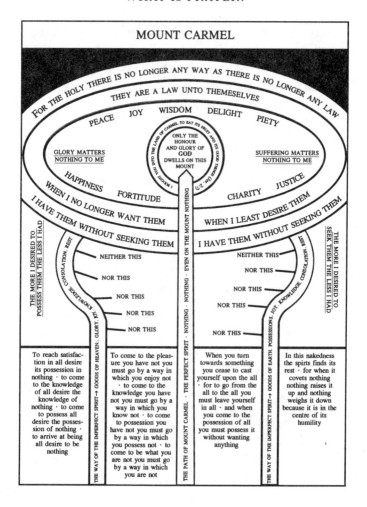

'Nothing', *nada*, is the space into which everything can flow. To make space for 'Totality', *todo*, no separate thing can be possessed. The 'nothing' of St John of the Cross is not a vacuum but a negating of the limited. If I attach myself to the limited, I close myself to the unlimited. Only this 'all' can give us full joy, full knowledge, full satisfaction.

St John's main reason for detachment is based on the infinite capacity of the human heart. Only the 'all' can really satisfy so St John virtually says, 'Don't stop short at the created – go beyond!' This teaching is beautifully distilled in his four-line *Suma de la perfección* or *Summary of perfection* (*Poems p. 108*):

> *Olvido de lo criado*
> *Memoria del Criador*
> *Atención a lo interior*
> *Y estarse amando al Amado.*
> Ignoring the created and inferior;
> Remembering above all things the Creator;
> Attention to the life that is interior;
> For the Beloved love that's always greater.

The intense personal urgency of his longing for union with God is expressed in a love poetry still unrivalled.

Note the triple imperative of our first quotation (from the *Song Between Soul and Bridegroom*) used within the already assured one-to-One rapport. In such a relationship of utter simplicity and truth no refusal is possible: 'Give me... send me... do not tell me – but – at once Thyself... no more a messenger...'. We have met 'Something' like this before?

> In God alone be at rest my soul. (*Pss 61.1 & 62*)

And

> God of your goodness give me Yourself...
> in You alone do I have all (*Revelations of Divine Love*)

This is the Way of the Ascended Man of Prayer, 'if you will,' in a shared One-to-one praying faith. But – in this present life it must be the *via negativa*: the way of the Cross; His way in us, refining our suffering into a Love beyond our unaided comprehension. In this Love, 'My God, my God, why have You forsaken Me?' is also in Unison with 'O Darkness lovelier than the dawn' (*Song of the Soul in Rapture*). In these now shared existential 'depthless caverns of awareness' (*Living Flame of Love*) the one 'Darkness' of soul is seen as 'Transfiguring them each into the other' –

Amado con amada
Amada en el Amado transformada!

I believe this is what is called transformation in Christ.

St John's love poetry came from his heart-to-Heart before the *Ascent of Mount Carmel* came from his head. The illative sense of this statement allows me to suggest (there must be at least an inner smile of recognition in heaven?) that *now* there is a perfect rapport between not only the English Mystics and St John of the Cross but also between the Carmelite Father John de Yepes and John, Cardinal Newman. Within the 'vein of the Gospel proffer' there is One spiritual Blood transfusion which allows, 'if you will', the teaching of the *Ascent of Mount Carmel* and the *Grammar of Assent* to be read as the *Assent of Mount Carmel* and the *Grammar of Ascent, mutatis mutandi*. For when the heart and the head work together in the one Body of Christ which is His Church, all people of good-will explore together the nature of belief. Herein, belief is an act of apprehension; subjective in character, incapable of logical proof but rational. We do not

reach certainties by logic but by intuitive perception.   There are those who await the canonisation of
Doctor Newman.   On becoming a Cardinal he chose
for his motto *Cor ad cor loquitur* – Heart speaks unto
heart.   Herein is the 'vein of the Gospel proffer'.

I. *Example IX: Seventeenth Century*
     Had you not found Me
     you could not now be seeking Me.   (*Pensées*)

Comment
The gift of intuitive perception is exactly what freed
Blaise Pascal from the *ennui* and *impasse* of his own
intellectualism.   In black despair he, probably the ablest
mathematician thinker of seventeenth century Europe,
records in his famous *Memorial* how: 'On Monday
23rd November 1654 between the hours of 10.30 and
12.30…' he tried to pray.   In this blackness a wordless
Voice spoke to him:

   Tu ne me chercherais pas, si tu ne me possedais.
   Had you not found Me
   you could not now be seeking Me.

From this restored at–One–ment with the Ascended

Man of Prayer flowed a joyful compunction of heart. Then with calm recollection he wrote down his *Magnificat*:

> God of Abraham, God of Isaac, not of philosophers and scholars… He can only be kept by ways taught in the Gospels… sweet and total renunciation, total submission to Jesus Christ.

J. *Example X*

> *Vacate et videte quoniam ego sum Deus*
> Be still and know that I am God (*Ps 45.6*)

> In God alone be at rest my soul (*Pss 61.1 62*)

Comment

Vacate, empty yourself of self to the point of utter stillness: then you will existentially 'see' into the *kenosis* of the Cross 'and know that I am God' (*Ps 45.6*).

The dynamics of grace illuminating our God-given freedom of choice draw us to see that His Love alone is necessarily '*semper agens, semper quietus*'. That we cannot be 'always active, always at rest' is the burden of our mortality. Only through at-One-ment with the Ascended Man of Prayer may we, as contingent beings, become fully aware that 'In God alone be at rest my soul' (*Pss 61.1 & 62*) is, truly, the innate desire of all of good-will. We are born with an insatiable desire for a final re-Union which we know cannot be obtained in this life alone. Even so, however transitory, the awareness of 'Something', 'I know not what…' gives us a 'Come on, We are in this together' or '*Dilectus meus mihi et ego Illi.*' And we then simply know we would not have things otherwise: '*Fiat*, let It be. I accept It needs must be so.'

K. Example XI

Dilectus meus mihi, et ego Illi… (*Song of Songs 6*)

Comment

'My Beloved to me, and I to Him' may be our first and, please God, our last, intimation of the indescribable implications of the Word Incarnate, living *now* among us. From the Beginning, One with the Father, the Ascended Man of Prayer is constantly revealing, through their one Advocacy a triune One-ness with us. In unison, *now*, we 'hear Him' always as though for the first time.

The Father loves me because I lay down my life in order to take it up again. No one takes it from me; I lay it down of my own free will, and as I have power to lay it down, so I have power to take it up again. (*Jn 10.18ff*)

Then the illative sense carries us on – This is my mandate from my Father for you so that 'all may be One'.

This is the mandate, of Perfect Com-mission, of the Father, freely offered to the Son, and freely taken by the Son, in the One Love which is their Spirit: 'My Beloved to Me, and I to Him.'

From our point of view, in prayer, we may see Their power of Love at work at the Last Supper. There His personal re-institution of this Original mandate which *now*, we recognise, as though for the first time, incorporates us from the Beginning. The washing of the feet and the giving of His Body and Blood show us the 'One thing necessary' – the Love of God, more intimately than ever before: 'My Beloved to me, and I to Him'.

It is simply incredible in human terms alone. But this is how he out-Faces sin and death in Gethsemane and on the Cross with perfect control and majestic calm. As he was, He is *now*, and for ever, *Rex tremendæ majestatis*; always ready for His second coming at the end of time. If we, now, with the Ascended Man of Prayer, persevere in prayer we shall in St Teresa's cheerful words, with our last breath, 'Enter and see we are already within.'

L. *Example XII*

With the drawing of this Love and voice of this Calling

> We shall not cease from exploration
> And the end of all our exploring
> Will be to arrive where we started
> And know the place for the first time.
> Through the unknown, remembered gate
> When the last of earth left to discover
> Is that which was the beginning;
> At the source of the longest river
> The voice of the hidden waterfall
> And the children in the apple-tree
> Not known, because not looked for
> But heard, half-heard, in the stillness
> between two waves of the sea.
> Quick now, here, now, always –
> A condition of complete simplicity
> (Costing not less than everything)
> And all shall be well and

> All manner of thing shall be well
> When the tongues of flame are in-folded
> Into the crowned knot of fire
> And the fire and the rose are one.
> (*TS Eliot, last lines of Little Gidding, Four Quartets*)

Comment

But what next? – the twelfth quotation? We've met it before, you may recall (page 17) and we shall take it up again (page 114). Why not let it complete the central section so that it unifies in itself the two questions *What is Prayer?* and *What Next?* Or let it conclude the book? Place it where you will and you will always find it fits and overflows past and future because it is inspired by the ever-present Johannine: 'in my Beginning is my End'. The first eight lines *echo* and approximate *St John's Prologue*; and the last three lines his *Apocalypse*: 'In my End is my Beginning'. There is a persistent Presence in the *Four Quartets*. It is apparent in the concluding lines quoted here. It defies any attempt at final analysis. It is simply there Calling for a One-to-one rapport:

> And the end of all our exploring
> will be to arrive where we started
> And know the place for the first time.

PART TWO

SECTION 4: WHAT NEXT?

From our earliest being and within our first physical and psychological movements we register this question: what next? Before we can speak we make it clear we are anticipating the next feed. Toddlers are great explorers. Nursery and primary school children are encouraged to 'grow-up' by question and answer. And when we think we are 'grown-up' we pride ourselves on our art of anticipation. The responsible adult world depends on forward planning. Yet, inexorably, our every next is *now*. Paradoxically this *now* is the only constant in our transitoriness. We may have momentary awareness of this truth; for example, either as 'the sacrament of the present moment' (*de Caussade, Self-Abandonment to Divine Providence*) or as we suffer the illusion that we may escape self in some form of transcendental meditation or 'fix'. Pressurised by temporality as the Jewish leaders (and the Apostles) were, they could not, despite the example and teaching of our Lord, Man of Prayer, make the vital connexion between their own 'what next?' and the transcendental *now* of the Resurrection which has to be for ever.

Two thousand years later we register both the initial

stress and the transforming joyous wonder of the forty days from Easter Sunday to His Ascension. Our prayerful attempts to respond to the Resurrection may be revelatory in more senses than we can at first realise. At one moment we are inspired by the accounts of His appearances as recorded in the *Acts*; the letters of St Peter and of St Paul; in the four gospels; and by the example and teaching of countless others (then and *now*), trying to identify with Him. The next moment there seems no connexion between past and present. It is in just such moments of grace that we can grow in faith, that is, faith-in-prayer, a praying faith. This is the unspoken 'Come' of the ever-present Man of Prayer, to Peter and to us (*Mt 14.28*). With the father of the epileptic demoniac we have to make first an act of faith in prayer despite our feelings: 'Lord, I do believe, help my unbelief' (*Mk 9.25*). Or, again, with Bartimæus, the blind beggar, our whole being cries out, 'Lord, that I may see again' (*Mk 10.46*).

Like the Apostles and disciples we can be incredulous if not inert. Herein we are brought face-to-Face with the truth: even in this seemingly impossible contradiction in terms He is always present. Every appearance of the risen Christ gave, and must continue to give, an increase of faith in Him. Eventually they recognised Him as the same Person but, somehow, more so. No longer confined by their memories of Him in terms of time and space, they could at last see Him and, as though for the first time, at-One-with-the-Father. Was their (and our) initial failure to recognise the resurrected One because, first, 'something' inside every human heart must freely recognize that Like seeks like? Did He not provide for this gift of recognition when He said: 'Let Us make man in our own image and likeness' (*Gen 1.26ff*)?

So, now, what is this 'something'? Is it a twinge of conscience? A self-block gap between Infinity and my existential finitude? An indescribable sense of emptiness? Or a restorative focus of grace which transforms 'nowhere' into *now*-here? St John reminds us of the answer:

Something which has existed since the Beginning... the Word, Who is Life – this is our subject. (*I Jn 1.1ff*)

Yes... but, what next? Surely what I need is a new crash course in Christology? Yes, but... even the pagan humanists and the materialist atheists can get degrees in theology these days. You don't have to be a believer to teach religion, do you? How about Christophany with an A? That is, the study of Christ not just as yet another academic subject, but as a personal desire to meet 'something', some One, Who speaks to me of His divinity as it is manifested in human terms. Compare and contrast this innate desire with the journey of the Magi in what we call His Epiphany. Yes, but… and it went on didn't it, the massacre of infants, and the flight into Egypt; and today?

Might it be, just might it be, that this 'something' which is our subject cannot be researched on our own terms alone? Is this not made man-i-fest, Man-in-Flesh, in the Incarnate Word as each and every one of good will tunes in by listening, at least with the baptism of desire, to what is called Christophony with an O? Compare, contrast and relate this to what we mean by 'symphony' and we have, at last, not only the joyous simplicity of the 'O and A' Christmas carol *Unto us is born a Son* … but 'something' totally and gloriously Comprehensive.

If we are 'at home' with our Lord Jesus Christ as Ascended Man of Prayer, we can, like Him, be *in* time but not *of* it. We may note glimpses of this now ageless fullness of reality in multifarious ways. For example, listen to this with the ear of your heart:

> When the appointed time came, God sent his Son, born of a woman, born a subject of the Law, to redeem the subjects of the Law and to enable us to be

adopted as sons. The proof that you are sons is that God has sent the Spirit of his Son into our hearts: the Spirit that cries, '*Abba*, Father,' and it is this that makes you a son, you are not a slave any more; and if God has made you a son, then He has made you heir.
(*Gal 4.4ff*)

Or, see the ageless Christophany manifest in stained glass from earliest times to the present day? For years I looked at a medieval trefoil medallion of stained glass *shewing* (*cf Julian's Shewings*) God the Father presenting to us on His outstretched arms God the Son crucified. Then, one day, by the gift of a new focus, I recognised that what I had mistaken as the long white beard of the Father was the artist's attempt to portray the Presence of the Holy Spirit in the form of a dove, wings swept back, streaming from the Son to the Father: 'Father, into your hands I commit my Spirit' (*Lk 23.46*). Then, I recognised that there was no age difference between the Father's look and that of the Son, in the triune God.

Until recently I have not liked the sound of 'atonement'. Mercifully, one day it was spelt out for me as at-One-ment. This now translates the haunting sound of a first cock-crow from remorse to compunction of heart. You will understand what I mean by this if you can see how Jesus must have looked at Peter. 'And he went out-side and wept bitterly' (*Mt 26.75*; *Mk 14.72*; *Lk 22.61*; *Jn 18.25*). This heart-cry cannot be put into words because only Christ can 'read' it for us to the Father. In this experiential recognition, in this Heart-to-heart, 'something' has become the Subject of the Last Supper, the Ascension, Pentecost; and His second and final com-ing at the end of time.

Meanwhile? The question, 'what next?' will not, thank God, go away. It keeps us in touch with Him with-in the Communion of Saints, known and unknown, as we try to listen in to what must, in this life alone, sound like the most poignantly unfinished 'symphony'. Let it speak to us:

I am soft sift
In an hourglass – at the wall
Fast, but mined with a motion a drift,
And it crowds and it combs to the fall;
I steady as a water in a well, to a poise, to a pane,
But roped with, always, all the way down from the tall
Fells or flanks of the voel, a vein
Of the gospel proffer, a pressure, a principle, a Christ's gift.

WHAT IS PRAYER?

I kiss my hand
To the stars, lovely-asunder
Star-light, wafting him out of it; and
Glow, glory in thunder;
Kiss my hand to the dappled-with-damson west;
Since, tho' he is under the world's splendour and wonder,
His mystery must be instressed, stressed;
For I greet him the days I meet him,
and bless when I understand.

Not out of his bliss
Springs the stress felt
Nor first from heaven (and few know this)
Swings the stroke dealt –
Stroke and a stress that stars and storms deliver,
That guilt is hushed by, hearts are flushed by and melt –
But it rides time like riding a river
(And here the faithful waver, the faithless fable and miss).

It dates from day
Of his going in Galilee;
Warm-laid grave of a womb-life grey;
Manger, maiden's knee;
The dense and the driven Passion, and frightful sweat;
Thence the discharge of it, there its swelling to be,

Though felt before, though in high flood yet –
What none would have known of it,
only the heart being hard at bay.
(*Wreck of the Deutschland, stanzas 4-7, GM Hopkins SJ*)

This 'vein of the gospel proffer, a pressure, a principle, a Christ's gift' is constantly with us (see *Jn 15.1* 'I am the Vine-vein…'). It is timeless yet we can experience it *now*. We are drawn to it again and again. We can recognise it at work in a strictly chronological order through the centuries and at the same time gather an awareness that it was in the Beginning before time began. It transcends time and 'it rides time like riding a river.' So, 'I greet Him the days I meet Him, and bless when I understand.' That might take us back to see our need of Him in our attempts to pray. 'And here the faithful waver, the faithless fable and miss.'

Perhaps, now, a closer, more reflective, look again at Julian of Norwich on prayer in her *Revelations of Divine Love* might help? Or, at least, consider again, very slowly, the offered excerpts? Let her prayer speak for us and within us:

God, of your goodness give me yourself, for you are sufficient for me. I cannot properly ask anything less, to be worthy of you. If I were to ask less, I should always be in want. In you alone do I have all.

You will find this in the penultimate paragraph of her fifth chapter, not as a separate, set prayer but as an integral part of her prayer life. What that meant to her and how she shared it with others is the book itself. She could not have written other than by the experience of grace.

In the excerpts from Julian's specific teaching on prayer (page 55*ff*), it seems to me, we are taken into the Heart of 'something' we all long for. It is, 'to know the goodness of God… that he loves the soul he has made in his own likeness… it surpasses all knowledge.' Yet, 'I now see [understand] what our Lord minded me of: "I am the foundation of your praying"… how can you not have what you ask for? He wills that we should have a true knowledge of himself that he is all-being.' And so, on to the climax: 'Prayer unites [oneth] the soul to God.' This must be the prayer of silent adoration – 'when the Holy Spirit touches the soul, it longs for God rather like this: "God, of your goodness give me yourself…"' This prayer, her every attempt to pray, her life of prayer, witness to the truth: 'God is love, they who live in love live in God and he lives in them' (*I Jn 4.16*).

Julian lived in fourteenth century England, the Age of

Chaucer and *The Canterbury Tales*. It was also the time of twice yearly visitations of the Black Death. Church and State seemed to be, to many then, and *now*, beyond redemption. Yet it produced Julian and several others known as the fourteenth century English mystics. This vein of the Vine… (*Jn 15.1*), their spiritual resilience, inspires us still because it *echoes* the authentic touch 'of the gospel proffer… a Christ's gift.'

Julian's book is clearly inspired by a warm-hearted gratitude for Christ's love as she recognises it in:

i   the distinction and excellence of our creation,

ii   the price and value of our redemption,

iii everything created has been put under us to serve us, and is upheld by him out of love for us.

In this way it is as though she is saying:

See, I have done all this long before your prayers; and *now* you exist, and pray to me. He means that we ought to know that the greatest deeds are already done, as Holy Church teaches. Gratefully realising this we ought to be praying for the deed *now* in process, which is that he should rule and guide us in this life for his own glory, and bring us to his bliss. (*p. 127*)

Julian's prayer life was, first, essentially Scriptural. Not above doubt and anxiety, she recognised, even in her worst fears and trials, the primacy of God's love for us. 'In the beginning was the Word' (*Jn 1.1ff*)... and, 'God loved us first' (*I Jn 4.16*) was *shewn* to Julian (and us) in his Passion ('if He could have suffered more for us He would have done so'). This Love alone triumphs over sin and death. 'It unites [oneth] the soul to God' and is therefore essentially and always Trinitarian. Such a love is encountered in prayer. And in prayer we can recognise that:

  i   the worst and the greatest has already happened,

  ii   that Love *is* stronger than death,

  iii   that by His Incarnation, Passion, Death, Resurrection and Ascension He gives us an atonement which can be at-One-ment even *now* and where this *now* is for ever, iv that therefore there can be no such thing as unanswered prayer,

v that prayer is primarily concerned with God, not with need. 'In God alone be at rest, my soul'. (*Pss 61.1 & 62*).

This recognition, so simple and so theologically profound, is not the result of academic study. It was only after twenty years of praying through and with Our Lord, Ascended Man of Prayer, in His *shewings* of divine love that she could bring herself to attempt to hand on what she had contemplated and simply because 'Love is the only answer'.

The answer she gives as follows:

page 70: The love of God for the soul surpasses all knowledge.

page 137: The whole of life is grounded and rooted in His love.

page 172: It is a love that cannot, will not, be broken by sin because It is rock-like.

page 193: It is the will of God that of all the qualities

of the blessed Trinity, that we should be most sure of, and delighted with, it is love. Love that makes might and wisdom come down to our level.

page 196: This is the threefold longing of God to share his love with us.

page 208: The whole strength of the *Revelations* depends on understanding three attributes of God, that he is life, love and light.

page 210: So that we love God for Himself, and love ourselves in God, and love what God loves, for His sake.

page 211: Because God is love, It is always Trinitarian and revealed in Christ. It is Infinite, Ineffable [beyond speech], Inviolable [unalterable] and the only constant: unchanging God, change-able [change-able] man.

When the disciples said, 'Lord, teach us to pray…' (*Lk 11. 1ff*), Our Lord, Man of Prayer did not first give a dissertation on different kinds of prayer. The 'Our Father' does not mention nor distinguish between vocal, mental or contemplative prayer. It is always timeless, immediate and simply perfect. It transcends time and space even as it epitomises His mission and our vocation. So, Julian writing up her reflections on the twelfth revelation (*chapter 26*) with still four to go, records:

> The extent of what he had to say was altogether beyond my capacity to understand or take in. As I see it, his words are the greatest that can be uttered, for they embrace… I cannot tell! All I know is that the joy I saw in that revelation surpasses all the heart could wish for or the soul desire. So let not those words be recorded here, but let each receive them as our Lord intended them, according to the grace God gives him for understanding and loving. (*p. 102*)

Julian, woman of prayer, in her anchor-hold, was, as we say, 'one with' our Lord, Ascended Man of Prayer. So too was her anonymous contemporary, the author of *The Cloud of Unknowing* (*Image Books 1973*). One guess is that he was a busy parish priest in North Yorkshire, but first and foremost he was a man of prayer. This is evident in his written attempts to answer the unending longing for God which he and all of us are born with. So

with our Lord, Ascended, Man of Prayer and our
unknown author we pray:

> O God unto whom all hearts lie open
> unto whom desire is eloquent
> and from whom no secret thing is hidden;
> purify the thoughts of my heart
> by the outpouring of your Spirit
> that I may love you with a perfect love
> and praise you as you deserve. Amen.

What next?

> In the name of the Father
> and of the Son and of the Holy Spirit.
> My dear friend in God,
> I would like to pass on to you
> what I have roughly observed
> about the Christian life. (p. 43)

God created us in his image and likeness, making us
like himself, and in the Incarnation he emptied himself of his divinity becoming a man like us. It is God,
and he alone, who can fully satisfy the hunger and
longing of our spirit which transformed by his

redeeming grace is enabled to embrace Him by love.
He whom neither men nor angels can grasp by
knowledge can be embraced by love. For the intel-
lect of both men and angels is too small to comprehend God as he is in himself. Try to understand this
point. Rational creatures such as men and angels possess two principal faculties, a knowing power and a
loving power. No one can fully comprehend the
uncreated God with his knowledge; but each one,
in a different way, can grasp him fully through love.
Truly this is the unending miracle of love: that one
loving person, through his love, can embrace God
whose being fills and transcends the entire creation.
And this marvellous work of love goes on for ever, for
He whom we love is eternal. Whoever has the grace
to appreciate the truth of what I am saying, let him
take my words to heart, for to experience this love is
the joy of eternal life while to lose it is eternal tor-
ment. (*p. 50*)

So, 'my dear friend in God', you see how within our
attempts at prayer we 'greet Him the days we meet Him,
and bless when we understand'. This is only possible
because in some way beyond our finite comprehension,
God alone constantly offers that perfect friendship we

long for. Our desire for this may be evoked as it is temporarily reflected in the good, the true, and the beautiful. But It can only be found in 'the gospel proffer, a pressure, a principle, a Christ's gift'. It can only be fully realised and retained in and with our Lord, Ascended Man of Prayer, who is the Way, the Truth and the Life (*Jn 14.6*). Did He not say, 'I call you friends because I have made known to you everything I have learnt from my Father' (*Jn 15.15*)? Just when they were experiencing that fear of separation, and that sense of 'gap' common to us all; just when we most feel the need of true friendship, His friendship? Witness how, even mistakenly, it is often talked about and sought after in terms of 'a very special and/or a very spiritual friend.' I think it transcends all definition. And this is why it is not just for this life alone.

At the end of *The Cloud of Unknowing* we read:

St Augustine explains what I mean by holy desire when he says 'The entire life of a good Christian is nothing less than holy desire.' My dear friend, I bid you farewell now… May God give you and all who love him true peace, wise counsel, and his own interior joy in the fullness of grace.

Surely this lovely valediction in some way *echoes* the

indescribable poignancy of our Lord's farewell to His disciples (and us) at the Last Supper (*Jn 16.7ff*) and at His Ascension (*Mt 28.19ff*).

In so far as I may understand any awareness of His friendship, the author of *The Cloud* re-*present*-s a distillation of this spirituality in his *Book of Privy Counselling*. It follows *The Cloud* in the *Image* edition beginning at *page 149*.

> It will feel as if your whole desire cried out for God and said:

>> That which I am I offer to you, O Lord, without looking to any quality of your being but only to the fact that you are as you are; this, and nothing more... that which I am, I offer to you O Lord, for you are it entirely. (*p. 150ff*)

In this way, His Way, His friends may recognise that

> Whatever we may say of it is not it, but only about it... Man's highest perfection is union with God in consummate love, a destiny so high, so pure in itself, and so far beyond human thought that it cannot be known or imagined as It really is. (*p. 169*)

It is this awareness of inexpressible 'blind love'; that moves St John of the Cross to cry out: 'Give me at once yourself; send me no more a messenger who cannot tell me what I wish…' and within that same 'blind' awareness to address the One out cry Itself as, 'O Darkness lovelier than the dawn,' and as it is experienced 'in depthless caverns of awareness.' (*St John of the Cross, Poems*).

It is true that there are numerous *echoes* between the fourteenth-century anonymous English prose writer and the world famous sixteenth-century Spanish poet and Doctor of the Church. I believe scholars try to explain this by reminding us that both were steeped in the Scriptures and shared a common ground in familiarity with the writings of pseudo-Dionysius. Basically it just might be as simply timeless and universal as: 'My Beloved to me, and I to Him…' (*Song of Songs chapter VI*). Or again within the experience and example of our Lord, Ascended Man of Prayer: 'Empty yourself [of self to the point of utter stillness] and see that I am God' (*Pss 45.11 & 62; Lk 24.46; Jn 19.30; Phil 2.5*).

If you will look again now at the pages of quotations from the first to the twentieth centuries and review them in so far as may help our attempt to answer the two questions *What is Prayer?* and *What Next?* we may find that both questions find One answer. The following points occur in common in the ever present research for a 'something': 'I know not what':

1. an I-Thou relationship between God and a soul in grace expressed in Incarnational terms which lead to a common-Union, a One-ness, which is essentially both human and divine. No relationship can be more truly intimate.

2. This relationship is, first, God's gift. It draws us to respond because Like seeks like.

3. The quotations reveal Love rather than knowledge: 'God loved us first.'

4. They express a longing 'I know not what' because it cannot be put into words. Only It can satisfy this longing *now* and therefore for ever.

5. They remind us, constantly, of His *now* in the given circumstances, including daily problems, pain, contradictions, *etc.*, yet still they offer *Pax inter spinas* – peace amongst thorns – because 'In His will is our peace.'

6. They all posit strong enduring personal friendship based on a shared prayerful awareness that 'the Heart has Its reasons'.

7. Although they are all from the past which is ever present, they help us advert to the eternal time-less-ness of God who is Emmanuel, God-with-us in the one community of all of good-will (God-will).

8. Prayer is the God-given desire of the individual to communicate with Him. It is a longing for at-One-ment: 'Prayer oneth the soul to God,' in and with the Ascended Christ, Who is always with us as Man of Prayer.

All these quotations, references, and comments singly or together, with any others we may prefer should, as they *echo* His scriptural prayer (especially of the Last Supper, *Jn 17.3 ff*) call us back to want to *be* eternally at home with Him.

The longing prepares us for each and every *fiat*, at whatever cost, so that we may home-in on, and resonate, the joy of the first *Magnificat*, because we are now and for ever, one Body in and with the Ascended Man of Prayer who is always with us.

But still we ask 'what next?' Are we afraid that, rather like some pictures of the Ascension show, we are supposed to be looking up at a cloud with, protruding from it, two pierced feet, suspended in space? Did not the Truth Himself say:

> It is necessary for you that I go [*Jn 16.7*] meaning, as St Augustine says: 'Were not the form of His human-ity withdrawn from our bodily eyes, love of Him in His Godhead would never cleave to our spiritual eyes'... in spiritual experience of God's love.
> (*The Book of Privy Counselling p. 187*)

> So I clothed myself in an ordinary human nature and made myself utterly available so that no one could excuse himself from coming because he did not know the Way. In my humanity, I am the door [*Jn 10.9*] and whoever comes in by way of me shall be safe.
> (*The Book of Privy Counselling p. 175*)

Safe? Yes, until the next doubt and fear. So it was with the Apostles and disciples, you remember; and so it is with us, even after two thousand years of further testimonies and confrontations between 'seeing is believing' and 'believing is seeing'. When we, like Mary Magdalene; the ten Apostles; the two disciples on the road to Emmaus, use only our physical sight we (like them) cannot see His ever present corporeality. But when we (like them) use our faith we recognise the Real Presence of His risen glorified Body, which, without faith seems like nothing but a physical absence. With con-*fid*-ence, that is, with-shared-faith in the Resurrection, we can re-call and enter into His demonstration of the Truth itself as foretold at the Last Supper. And 'This' was re-*present*-ed in the Upper Room on Easter evening. After initiating the Holy Sacrament of His Body and Blood at the Last Supper, He had said 'I will not eat and drink with you again until in the Kingdom' (*Mt 26.29*; *Mk 14.25*; *Lk 22.16*). *Now*, here, three days later, He is eating and drinking with them.

As we communicate today He is with us as He was with the ten on Easter evening. Earlier he had said in His preaching: 'the Kingdom of heaven is already within you' (*Lk 17.20*). For this to be true, *now*, we have to accept an utterly profound, simple, change of heart and mind wherein 'seeing is believing' becomes 'believing is seeing' according to His word; Incarnate and Ascended, yet ever Present.

We must constantly try to recapitulate what it means

now to live as One-in-and-with the Ascended Christ, Man of Prayer:

First, the significance of this must be recognised as a growing awareness, *in via*. It begins on earth as we pray with our Lord, Ascended Man of Prayer, and goes on for ever. Ascended and *now* in glory, He is the full *term** of the Second Person (of the Blessed Trinity) in One human and divine *be*-ing. Already we can, by faith, recognise Him as the same Person of the Last Supper and the Upper Room, but, even more so. This is part of the ever present *now* of the Resurrection.

It is always difficult to believe this because we have no experience of *be*-ing as an ageless person in a body not limited by time and space. We can anticipate what this means if we identify with Him at prayer on Mount Tabor during His transfiguration (*Mt 17.1; Lk 9.28*) or listen to His instruction given to explain the state of *be*-ing enjoyed by the resurrected 'living as the angels are' (*Lk 20.27ff*) and '*Now* he is God, not of the dead, but of the living; for to Him all are in fact alive.' Therefore we are naturally incredulous, like Mary Magdalene; the ten Apostles; the two disciples on the Emmaus road; and finally the eleven; even after several Appearances (*Jn 21.1ff*). These very

---

*   See pp 15, 42, 50 & 52.

failures to recognise Him became for them, and can become for us, also, moments of clearer recognition of the Truth Itself.

Three areas for prayerful reflection may increase this gift of recognition:

1. First, remembered, re-*present*-ed signs or incidents gave them and can give us, greater joy than ever experienced before. For example, just His saying 'Mary' (*Jn 20.16*); the blessing and breaking of the Bread at Emmaus (*Lk 24.14*); the triple affirmation of Peter (*Jn 21.15*); but, surely for us, *now*, the reply to doubting Thomas: 'you believe because you can see Me, but more blessed are they who have not seen, yet believe' (*Jn 20.29*).

2. Secondly, the, so to speak, indescribable sadness and joy: the pain of separation and the longing for Union that must accompany a Christian death. It has to be experienced in order 'to see' that His love *is* stronger than death. In His Death, Resurrection and Ascension we *now* cannot, in our Christian death, suffer an irreparable loss but instead we receive immeasurable grace: *Now* in my End is my beginning. As the *Preface for the Dead* in the

Roman Rite reminds us, 'life is changed, not ended.' The Ascended Christ, Man of Prayer, prompts us in the Holy Spirit with His constant Compassion: 'you are sad now, but I shall see you again, and your hearts will be full of joy' (*Jn 17.22*).

3. Thirdly, His confrontation with everything alien to and insufficient for the spiritual in us terrifies and up-lifts us as we recognise the Ascended as *Rex tremendæ majestatis*, and always as the same Person but more so: we remain incredulous while we grow in faith. '*Caro cardo salutis*': Yes, *now*, 'the Flesh is the door-hinge of Salvation.'

And, yes, after two thousand years of further testimonies and confrontations we still 'waver' and 'fable and miss' as we cling to this earth so eloquent of Him:

I see His Blood upon the rose,
And in the stars the glory of His eyes. (*JM Plunkett*)

Only He Himself is sufficient for us.

When we like Mary Magdalene; the eleven; the two on the Emmaus road, use only our physical sight and our own finite thinking, we cannot recognise his Real

Presence. When we, like them, use our faith He is with us as He was with them. In this vitally important change of heart and mind believing is seeing that we can eat and drink with Him and all of good-will (God will) daily. Then we see ever more clearly that what we may experience in this 'Connexion' as 'separation' is in fact a Communion outside of which there is no greater Reality. 'It is for your own good that I am going (or coming) because unless I go the Advocate will not come to you' (*Jn 16.22*). Had He not ascended we could not see that our every next is *now* as we enter into the divine Context of His creative redemptive Love wherein *now* is for ever.

We begin again, and as though for the first time, as we pray in and with our Lord, Ascended Man of Prayer, to recognise our shared vocation: to live *now* in the Spirit. So we pray again and again:

Come, O Holy Spirit,
fill the hearts of Your faithful
and enkindle in them the fire of your Love.
Send forth your Spirit and they shall be created.
And You shall renew the face of the earth.

and again

O God, who taught the hearts of the faithful
by the light of the Holy Spirit,
grant that by the gift of the same Spirit
we may be always truly wise
and ever rejoice in His consolation.

We make our prayer through Christ our Lord,
in the one Holy Spirit,
to the glory of God the Father.

And herein, always, 'the glory of God is man fully alive'
(*St Irenæus, Second Century*).

Christ's Ascension is our guarantee that one day we
will be completely 'at home' with Him if we believe in
the power of His Resurrection. The whole life of the
Church suffering and yet redeemed inheres between the
Ascension and His return on the last day. Meanwhile,
the One Word statement must be the answer to all our
questions, as the Scriptures constantly remind us:

The Word of God is Something alive and active: it cuts
like any double-edged sword but more finely: it can
slip through the place where the soul is divided from
the spirit, or joints from the marrow; it can judge
the secret emotions and thoughts. No created thing

can hide from Him; everything is uncovered and open to the eyes of the One to Whom we must give account of ourselves.

Since in Jesus, the Son of God, we have the supreme high priest Who has gone through to the highest heaven, we must never let go of the faith that we have professed. For it is not as if we had a high priest who was incapable of feeling our weaknesses with us; but we have One who has been tempted in *every* way that we are, though He is without sin. Let us be confident, then, in approaching the throne of grace, that we shall have mercy from Him and find grace when we are in need of help. (*Hebrews 4.12ff*)

In all possible simplicity and truth, to pray is to live. But how do I know? The truth is, experience teaches us. It is infinitely simple: *ad-oro Te, ergo sum.* Yes, at this moment I turn to You in prayer, I pray to You, therefore I am. So we recognise You in the desire You give us to adore You, O Christ and to bless You

as Ascended Man of Prayer : *Magnificat.*

Word–in–the–womb–of–time : *Magnificat.*

WHAT NEXT?

You intercede for us : *Magnificat.*

All our hope is in You : *Magnificat.*

You are now, and for ever : *Magnificat.*

CONCLUSION

As we know, this wonderful hope cannot be fully realised in this life alone. We are contingent beings and although fallen we are redeemed. Therefore we must pray constantly for our right response to His healing Presence. In this way, His Way, 'in Him we live and move and have our being.' (*Acts 17.28*). For the *present* it has to be for all of us, a shared pilgrimage made possible in the Spirit of the Ascended. With Him we can experience a reconciliation between the seemingly irreconcilable contradiction of freedom of choice and dependence upon Him as Ascended Man of Prayer. With this gloriously humbling inter-dependent Pray-er rests our chief dignity as stewards of His new, and constantly re-newing, creation (*II Cor 5.17ff*). As we pray and work with Him at this reconciliation we are constantly reminded of His and our need to give primacy to prayer by the countless witnesses of the pray-ers who have gone before us. This is especially so with our Lady and all the saints. They, *now*, in fullest Communion with the Ascended Man of Prayer, ever irradiate with Him the Divine Mercy of God our Father. In this way we cannot help but long for and look forward to, *be*-ing at home within one Holy Family.

CONCLUSION

Do not let your hearts be troubled. Trust in God still, and trust in me. There are many rooms in my Father's house; if there were not, I should have told you... I shall return to take you with Me so that where I AM you may be too.' (*Jn 14. 1ff*)

Yes, but that was before His Ascension: where is He *now*?

At the beginning of *Burnt Norton*, the first of the *Four Quartets*, TS Eliot invites us, if we will, to reflect with him on the nature of time and reality. Once when commenting on his poetry he said. 'Just listen. Don't try to analyse.' If we are receptive to this 'listening', intuitive perception may then be the reward for such sound advice. There's nothing trite in that, or this: Confucius said, 'Its always later than you think.' Eliot's kind of 'listening' expresses the living truth:

> .... human kind
> Cannot bear very much reality.
> Time past and time future
> What might have been and what has been
> Point to one End, which is always present.
> Unless we enter this kind of real 'listening'
> we shall miss...
> The still point of the turning world.

God is the only centre Point
and that Centre is everywhere.
……… And all is always *now*.

So we meet, again and again, in multifarious ways, the
Father's Christocentric Love pulling us back to where
we really want to be, centred in Him.

With the drawing of this Love
and the Voice of this calling
[echoing directly, The Cloud of Unknowing, chapter 2]
We shall not cease from exploration.
And the End of all our exploring
Will be to arrive where we started
And know the place for the first time.
Through the unknown, remembered gate
When the last of earth left to discover
Is that which was the Beginning:
[reverberating Jn 1.1ff]
At the source of the longest river
[reminiscent of John of the Cross:
Song between Soul and Bridegroom]
The voice of the hidden waterfall
And the children in the apple-tree
Not known, because not looked for

But heard, half-heard, in the stillness
[nada y todo – nothing becomes everything]
Between two waves of the sea.
Quick *now*, here, *now*, always –
A condition of complete simplicity
[via negativa, purification of soul, cf next line]
Costing not less than everything
[Neither choose nor refuse: complete detachment for
attachment to unum necessarium: the Love of God]
And all shall be well and
All manner of thing shall be well
[Julian, Revelations, chapter 27]
When the tongues of flame are in-folded
Into the crowned knot of fire
And the fire and the rose are one.

The last three lines resonate archetypal images and patterns which have an all-encircling apocalyptic resounding *now*-here.

From beginning to end, the *Four Quartets* convey a sense of 'I know not what' within a transcendental Presence. Listen, and let It, 'if you will…' speak to you in 'the stillness between two waves of the sea' of human 'reality'. If you really 'listen with the ear of your heart' you will already be praying, *in via*, on the Way.

.... If you came this way,
Taking any route, starting from anywhere,
At any time or at any season,
It would always be the same:

you would have to put off
sense and notion. You are not here to verify,
Instruct yourself, or inform curiosity
Or carry report. You are here to kneel
Where prayer has been valid. And prayer is more
Than an order of words, the conscious occupation
Of the praying mind, or the sound

of the voice praying.
And what the dead had no speech for, when living,
They can tell you, being dead: the communication
Of the dead is tongued with fire beyond

the language of the living.

We are bedevilled by time whenever we think we exist
extra to this ever present Communication of the living
and the dead.

Do you, by now, feel not only bedevilled by time but
also benighted with words? And now you are asked to
believe in a nameless Presence-Incarnate? Yes, 'The hint
half guessed, the gift half understood, is Incarnation.'

Are we not, here and *now*, after all, philandering with

neo-platonic platitudes 'where action… has in it no source of movement?'

'If you will…' and remember, we cannot not choose; yes, if you will return to the only Original Word and let it speak to you then you will be facing the Truth.

In the Beginning was the Word, and the Word was with God, and the Word was God. He was in the Beginning with God; all things were made through Him, and without Him was not anything made that was made. In Him was Life and this Life was the light of men. The Light shines in the Darkness, and the darkness comprehended it not. The true Light that enlightens every one was coming into the world, and the world was made through Him, yet the world knew Him not. He came to His own home, and His own people received Him not. But to all who received Him, who believed in His name, He gave power to become children of God; who were born, not of blood nor of the will of the flesh nor of the will of man, but of God. And the Word became flesh and dwelt among us, full of grace and truth; we have beheld His glory, glory as of the only Son from the Father… And from His fullness have we all received, grace upon grace… grace and truth came through

Jesus Christ. No one has ever seen God; the only Son, Who is within the Heart of the Father, He has made Him known. (*Jn 1.1-18*)

The Ascended Man of Prayer, 'who is in the Heart of the Father,' has made His choice, once and for all: His atone-ment for our at–One-ment, even *now*. Can you believe this? Do I believe this?

In any attempt to pray we are, we must be, *now* one with Him in heart and mind and purpose: *lex orandi, lex credendi* – the law of praying is the law of believing. Or, the Way of the Pray-er is the way of the faithful. In this praying-faith, shared with Him and all of good-will:

I trust and hope : *Magnificat.*

'Lord, I do believe, help my unbelief'
(*Mk 9.25*) : *Magnificat.*

'Courage, I have overcome the world
(*Jn 16.33*) : *Magnificat.*

'I AM with you always;' : *Magnificat.*

'Yes, to the End of time' : *Magnificat.*

CONCLUSION

So we begin again by asking our Lady to join her prayers (*cf Lk 1.26ff*) to ours:

> Hail Mary, full of grace, the Lord is with thee.
> Blessed art thou among women
> and blessed is the fruit of thy womb Jesus.
> Holy Mary, Mother of God, pray for us sinners,
> *now* and at the hour of our death. Amen.

In this prayer we catch again St Luke's account of the Annunciation and Visitation (*Lk 1.26ff*). We may experience, once again, the simple beauty and joy of that first perfectly human *fiat*. So we are moved to recognise that we share her vocation. That is, to draw others closer, not to ourselves, but to her Son.

Then we must add –

> Pray for us, O Holy Mother of God,
> that we may be made worthy
> of the promises of Christ.

And again the Psalmist speaks for us:

> *Suscipe me, Domine, secundum eloquium tuum, et vivam.*
> *Et non confundas me ab exspectatione mea.*

Take me, Lord, according to your Word and I shall live.
And then my hopes shall not be in vain. (*Ps 119*)

Fiat – yes, may it be so

God's judgement has to be one of love and mercy

Magnificat